OLYMPIC GAMES

BARCELONA
1992

Mosaik

The Italian Sacchi, Sadovyi and Diebel were in agreement. You can swim faster with a shaven head

Vitali Schterbo was one of the most successful athletes in Barcelona

The two golds for Britain in the rowing have given the sport a boost

Linford Christie - Britain's gold medallist in the 100 metres sprint

Torbjörn Kornbakk and Nestor Almanza struggle for supremacy in the Greco-Roman wrestling

Italian Giovanni Trillini won the gold medal in the women's foil

Contents

The German team in the road race on their way to gold

Piet Raymakers on Ratina was in the Dutch team which won gold in the show jumping

The American basketball 'dream team' lived up to their reputation, beating Croatia to take the gold

Foreword

One of the best Olympic Games ever! That verdict on Barcelona '92 is unanimous. The largest number of nations in the history of the Games met in an historic European city, famous for sun, sea and the arts. The world's best gave their best in pursuit of an Olympic ideal. The British sporting world will be proud of its gold medal winners: Linford Christie, for example, the fastest man in the world, or Sally Gunnell with her effortless hurdling style. Amongst Britain's 20 medals, there were also successes in cycling, judo, rowing, archery, yachting, canoeing and swimming. But the most satisfying feature of the XXV Olympiad was the absence of political boycotts. After 20 years of international wrangling, at least the sporting world can say to its political masters, "We can put our differences to one side." Another pleasing feature was the achievements of the smaller countries, such as Ethiopia or Morocco. It surprised no one that the richer nations who invest in training their youth did so well. Yet the smaller nations attracted the public's sympathies. And to add to the spectators' enjoyment, there was the unifying effect of the host country's splendid performance. Having hitherto won only four gold medals in the history of the Games, the Spanish people can be justifiably proud of the total of 13 golds. This unique record in words and pictures portrays one of the most successful sporting events of the post-war era. No television can give a better account of the 1992 Olympic Games.

The Greatest Spectacle on Earth

Under starter's orders

On 25 July 1992, the Games of the XXV Olympiad came under starter's orders. The training was done, the stadia ready and waiting and soon the gladiators would march to the tunes of glory. But first, millions around the world watched the opening ceremony. An archer stood on the stage in the Montjuic stadium. He fitted a burning arrow and angled his bow. His fingers slowly uncurled, sending the arrow flying to a giant torch high on the stadium wall. With a flash, the Olympic flame was lit and the Greatest Games on Earth had begun.

Fifteen days later, the men's marathon runners climbed the testing two-mile hill to the Montjuic stadium for a gruelling finale in a city where, in the blistering summer heat, just sitting in a flat turning the pages of a newspaper can seem like hard work.

The camera never lies

There were plenty of familiar faces, like Carl Lewis and Steffi Graf, new ones like German swimmer, Franziska van Almsick and the American gymnast, Shannon Miller. There were also many of the top British stars like Liz McColgan and Lynford Christie. There were petite Russians and giant-sized Bulgarians, horses and hockey, pitchers and putters among the cast of more than 10,000 in this great sporting arena. The memories will linger of the astonishingly supple girl gymnasts, the determined concentration of the big lifters, the taut mid-air tumblings of the platform diver – those demonstrations of magic from fearless athletes at the very pinnacle of their powers. Television can record and re-run those moments, but the camera can frame for posterity the colour and the beauty, the grace and the power, the dreams and the disappointment, the glory and the pain.

A spectacle within a spectacle

The spectacle of the XXV Olympiad took place within a spectacle itself – Barcelona. A city of culture and a city of dreams, undoubtedly it is one of Europe's most exciting attractions.

Issues such as drug abuse, the impartiality of the officials and the influence of the sponsors were also on the Olympic agenda.

The spectators had a lot of fun too!

Linford Christie made it to the very top. He is the only top-class European sprinter.

'Magic' Johnson charmed the crowds wherever he went.

Evgueni Sadovyi, one of the several shaved heads on view in the swimming pool, took three gold medals home.

As Spain's second city, and with a population of 1.7 million, there was still scarcely enough room to fit everyone in and, of course, everyone included not just the athletes, but officials, media representatives and volunteer stewards, not to mention spectators.

This year there were two new sports, badminton and baseball, bringing the number of official sports to 25. There was also a number of extra events, including women's judo, two more yachting competitions for women, a women's 10 km walk and four canoe-slalom events. The total number of medal events increased to 257, 20 more than in the 1988 Games, a record in itself.

As well as all the official events, there were three demonstration events. Traditionally, these sports should reflect some aspect of the host nation's sporting interests. Basque pelota, a sport which originates in the Basque region of France and Spain, is commonly played in the Spanish-speaking parts of the world and is a squash-type game, in which a hard ball is hit against a wall. Roller hockey was another of the demonstration sports. Simply explained, it is hockey on roller skates. Again, it is a popular Spanish game and one enjoyed by IOC President, Juan Samaranch, in his younger days. The third demonstration sport, taekwondo, was featured in Seoul and may soon achieve full recognition. A spectacular martial art, it is very popular in the Far East.

Lord of the rings

The preparations for 1992 started well beforehand. One of the city's leading citizens, a banker and former diplomat, Juan Antonio Samaranch, became President of the IOC in January 1981. The IOC chooses the cities where the Olympics are to be held and so it came as no surprise when, against five other cities, Samaranch announced to a meeting in the IOC's home town of Lausanne on October 17, 1986: "And the Games of the XXV Olympiad are awarded to Barcelona, Spain."

No losers in Barcelona

Unlike the hapless citizens of Montreal who are still paying for the privilege of having hosted the 1976 Games, nobody will have lost any money this time. The Olympic Games is now big business. There were no banners or boards, trademarks on sports equipment were discreet. Only Wimbledon keeps its sporting arena as commercially clean as the Olympic organisation.

More was written about Gail Devers' miraculous recovery from a serious illness than her victory in the 100 metres sprint.

The changing face of the Games

The years from Seoul to Barcelona witnessed a momentous period in world history. Moscow's hold on much of eastern Europe collapsed in the winter of 1989 and then, in the summer of 1991, the USSR itself disintegrated after an unsuccessful coup d'état. So amazingly, there was no Soviet Union and no East Germany. Between them, these two nations had won 92 gold medals in Seoul. The former republics of the Soviet Union made up the Commonwealth of Independent States and competed under the Olympic flag. After many years of division, there was one united German team.

Banished from the Olympic Games for over 30 years, South Africa was re-admitted, as the racial divisions of apartheid were slowly being dismantled. Joining South Africa after even longer absences, were the old Baltic republics and the former

Yugoslavian states. The citizens of these fledgling countries saw Barcelona as a historic national landmark, after long, and sometimes bloody, struggles for international recognition.

Looking ahead

Earlier this year, 12 of the former Soviet states were awarded provisional membership of the IOC. There are several other obvious candidates and who knows what is likely to happen to Europe's borders in the next four years. This proliferation of member states is just one of the headaches awaiting the IOC, as it comes to terms with the arithmetic for Atlanta 1996. There will just not be room for the fringe competitors or passengers in future Games. "It's all about excellence now," remarked one British official. It is an even greater irony to contemplate the challenge that faced Boris Becker and his fellow tennis professionals. Accustomed to playing for huge sums of money, they competed for a small golden disc.

Stefka Kostadinova couldn't quite match her German rival, Heike Henkel (above), in the high jump.

16-year-old Jennifer Capriata took the women's singles tennis gold beating Steffi Graf for the first time in five encounters.

Chris Boardman's aerodynamic bike aroused enormous interest. His gold medal in the 4,000 metres individual pursuit boosted the spirits of the British teams.

The Searle brothers, Johnny and Greg from Chertsey came from behind to win in exciting style. They won the coxed pairs guided by Garry Herbert.

Gareth Marriott (right) from Mansfield came within a whisker of taking gold in the C1 canoe slalom. He kneels in the canoe to get maximum power.

Simon Terry from Lincolnshire said it was the only thing he could do well. He won a bronze in the individual archery competition and helped his team to a bronze in the team competition.

The Barcelona Olympiad was a unique event in recent Olympic history. Whilst following the recent trend towards commercialism, this has certainly been one of the least acrimonious Games and, in every respect, can only be described as a spectacular success.

Two dramatic golds

The British performance in Barcelona will probably be remembered for two dramatic gold medals for which the captains of the men's and women's athletics teams were responsible. Linford Christie's gold in the 100 metres final was won with what looked like consummate ease. He powered through the heats, progressing easily to the final. Once there, he was not going to make any mistakes. The single-minded determination he demonstrated in his quest for the gold was obvious to those who saw the television pictures of his expression - at once, intense, aggressive and supremely confident. He wouldn't allow himself to be distracted by the false starts and won the final by a considerable margin. He became only the third British competitor in history to win the Olympic 100 metres.

At 32, he had left it late in life to produce such an amazing season, but he has managed to progress from being a mere medal contender to becoming the fastest man in the world and Olympic 100 metres champion.

New athletics heroine

The women's team captain, Sally Gunnell, became the first European to win a gold in a relatively new event for women, the 400 metres hurdles. The event was only introduced in 1984, having previously been deemed too demanding for women. Both Gunnell and Christie won by relatively large margins and both easily beat the American favourites. In Gunnell's case, that favourite was Sandra Farmer-Patrick, who is probably the faster of the two athletes. However, her style of running and hurdling was unimpressive in comparison to Gunnell's flowing movements. It was

Gunnell's day, and she took the gold for Britain.

Boardman's magnificent machine

In the first week of the Olympics, Britain picked up its first gold medal in cycling. Chris Boardman won the 4000 metres pursuit title. Not surprisingly, his bike captured as many headlines as the rider. It had been built by Lotus Engineering of Norwich, who had made use of some of NASA computers for the

Some surprises, some disappointments
The British team
had plenty to celebrate

aerodynamic work. Boardman's success on the bike will certainly provide an enormous boost to British racing bike design and manufacturing, even though Boardman's friends and rivals credited his win to his performance rather than his bike.

Swimming medals hard to find

Boardman's medal came at a good time for Britain, since the swimming events being held at the same time were a distinct disappointment. Adrian Moorhouse, perhaps Britain's most likely medallist in the swimming, finished last in the final of the men's 100 metres breaststroke. In the same race, Nick Gillingham, another possible medal contender, came second from last but managed to improve on this later in the week in the 200 metres breast stroke. His bronze was the only British medal for swimming in Barcelona, a disappointing performance for the largest and strongest team we had sent to Barcelona.

Three in a row for Redgrave

The rowing world have come to view the first week of the Olympics as traditional celebration for Steven Redgrave's gold medal. This was his third consecutive rowing medal. In 1984, he won the coxed pairs alongside Andy Holmes. In 1988, with the same partner, he won the coxless pairs, and this year, with a new partner, Matthew Pinsent, he retained his coxless pairs title, a feat all the more remarkable as he had spent much of the last year suffering from illness. The Searle bro-

thers, with their cox, Garry Herbert, won the coxed pairs, taking the title from the the much-fancied Italians in a last-minute spurt over the line. Not many events had such nail-biting finishes. There were silvers for Britain in canoeing and judo, with Britain just losing out on a gold medal once again in the latter. There were two bronze medals for Britain in the archery – one individual and one team. Simon Terry surprised himself in the singles 70 metres competition. Robble Reid took a creditable bronze in the light-middleweight boxing and was unlucky not to do better. He is now likely to turn professional.

Bronze galore

The women's hockey team took a bronze in their tournament, eclipsing the men, who could only finish sixth in the defence of their Seoul

Nick Gillingham had high hopes of the top prize in the 200 metres breaststroke. He won a bronze medal.

The first Briton in history to win a yachting medal in the Soling class: Lawrie Smith and his team, Rob Cruikshank and Ossie Stewart.

Boxer Michael Carruth, a triplet from south Dublin returned to the Emerald Isle with a gold medal. He beat the Cuban, Juan Hernandez in the welterweight.

The German swimmers congratulate the Americans - gold for the US and silver for the Germans.

Sergei Bubka (right), superstar polevaulter from the Unified Team, failed to take a medal in Barcelona.

Ray Stevens, a superb judoka, took a rare judo medal for Britain.

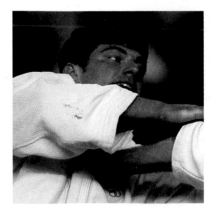

gold medal. Two bronze medals came from Sharon Rendle and Kate Howey in the women's judo. Another came in the yachting, thanks to the phlegmatic Lawrie Smith and his Soling class team. But it was in the athletics where the rest of the medals were won. Steve Backley had been suffering from too many injuries, but took a bronze in the javelin, while Kriss Akabusi finished his international career with two bronze medals in the 400 metres hurdles and in the 4 x 400 metres relay. In typical fashion, he was happy to have played his part in a world-record breaking race. Sally Gunnell took a bronze to supplement her earlier gold as a member of the 4 x 400 metres women's relay adding the finishing touches to Britain's medal haul.

Unhappy memories

There were, however, some major disappointments. Derek Redmond, having just recovered from one serious injury, looked to be in top form. However, a pulled hamstring in the semi-final robbed him of a medal and left us with one of the most abiding and poignant memories of the whole Games. He struggled around the rest of the course, supported by his father, who had come down from the stands and jumped over the barriers to be with his son in his misery.

One of the most disappointed athletes to leave Barcelona must have been the Scottish 10,000 metres runner, Liz McColgan. The threat to her title was perceived as coming from the South African, Elana Mey-

er, but McColgan knew that there were indeed a number of other challengers. By the end of the race, four women had finished in front of her, Lynn Jennings, a Chinese runner, Elana Meyer and the winner, Ethiopian Derartu Tulu.

A rising hope for the future of British track events, Dave Grindley, beat Redmond's British record and finished sixth in the final. The other half of Britain's new duo, Curtis Robb, finished in the same position in the 800 metres final. Both have future medal potential. Britain had three runners in the 110 metres final and Tony Jarrett just failed to take the bronze in a photo finish.

Irish boxing gold

One of the surprises and pleasures of the boxing tournament was the success of an Irish boxer by the name of Michael Carruth, who won the title in the welterweight class. In the final, he faced a Cuban, by the name of Juan Hernandez, who was expected to make light of the triplet from south Dublin. Suddenly and dramatically and amid some wild, roistering cele-

Moroccan, Khalid Skah incurred the derision of the crowd after winning the 10,000 metre. It was claimed that a fellow countryman had impeded his Kenyan challenger.

brations, Carruth was on the podium in the centre of the ring with the gold around his neck. There were some more celebrations in Dublin that night.

British athletes in disgrace

Unfortunately for Britain, one of the biggest drugs stories at these Games concerned British athletes. Sprinter Jason Livingston and two weightlifters, Andrew Saxton and Andrew Davies, were banned and sent home after testing positive for drugs, the tests having been conducted in Britain some ten days previously. All the men protested their innocence, the weightlifters admitting to taking an asthma drug to relieve asthma and chest pains. The rest of their defence relied on the fact that the drug itself is not on the list of banned substances. Livingston said that before the Games he was taking a form of vitamin/mineral supplement, which had been approved by the team doctor, and says he can only think that his sample had been tampered with. Although the British name was tarnished by the 'clenbuterol' affair, it was one of very few such incidents.

Enjoyable and efficient

The official media guide to the Games claimed that the 1992 Games were the 'the most brilliant games in modern Olympic history.' That was written weeks before the Games started. They have, for sure, been enjoyable and efficient. They passed without disasters, but without the emergence of any dominant personalities. One American magazine split its cover between Linford Christie and Gail Devers. Christie carried the Union Jack in the final parade. His win was certainly the most spectacular of Britain's five medals, exactly the same number of golds as the three previous Olympics. Further analysis of the medal's tables reveals that four fewer medals were won in Barcelona than in Seoul. "It's remarkable we do as well as we do," said Dick Palmer, general secretary of the British Olympic Association. "We've done well to hold on to our position. Standards are rising all the time. To stand still, we've got to invest more." Whether the Government has got the message, remains to be seen.

The victorious German cyclists celebrate Formula One style after winning the 100 kilometre team time trial (above).

Liz McColgan will have returned to Scotland disappointed after the 10,000 metres. She had been one of Britain's best medal hopes on the athletics track

German rider, Nicole Uphoff, wh took gold in the dressage, was moved by the medals ceremony.

Medals table

		Gold	Silver	Bronze	
1.	Unified Team/CIS	45	38	28	111
2.	USA	37	34	37	108
3.	Germany	33	21	28	82
4.	China	16	22	16	54
5.	Cuba	14	6	11	31
6.	Spain	13	7	2	22
7.	South Korea	12	5	12	29
8.	Hungary	11	12	7	30
9.	France	8	5	16	29
10.	Australia	7	9	11	27
11.	Italy	6	5	8	19
12.	Canada	6	5	7	18
13.	Great Britain	5	3	12	20
14.	Romania	4	6	8	18
15.	CSFR	4	2	1	7
16.	North Korea	4	–	5	9
17.	Japan	3	8	11	22
18.	Bulgaria	3	7	6	16
19.	Poland	3	6	10	18
20.	Kenya	2	4	2	8
21.	Netherlands	2	6	7	15
22.	Norway	2	4	1	7
23.	Turkey	2	2	2	7
24.	Indonesia	2	2	1	5
25.	Brazil	2	1	–	3
26.	Greece	2	–	–	2
27.	Sweden	1	7	4	12
28.	New Zealand	1	4	5	10
29.	Finland	1	2	2	5
30.	Denmark	1	1	4	6
31.	Morocco	1	1	2	4
32.	Ireland	1	1	–	2
33.	Ethiopia	1	–	2	2
34.	Algeria	1	–	1	2
35.	Estonia	1	–	1	2
36.	Lithuania	1	–	1	2
37.	Switzerland	1	–	–	1
38.	Jamaica	–	3	1	4
39.	Nigeria	–	3	1	4
40.	Latvia	–	2	1	3
41.	Namibia	–	2	–	2
42.	Austria	–	2	–	2
43.	South Africa	–	2	–	2
44.	Belgium	–	1	2	3
45.	IOP	–	1	2	3
46.	Iran	–	1	2	3
47.	Croatia	–	1	2	3
48.	Israel	–	1	1	2
49.	Mexico	–	1	–	1
50.	Peru	–	1	–	1
51.	Taiwan	–	1	–	1
52.	Mongolia	–	–	2	2
53.	Slovenia	–	–	2	2
54.	Argentina	–	–	1	1
55.	Bahamas	–	–	1	1
56.	Ghana	–	–	1	1
57.	Qatar	–	–	1	1
58.	Colombia	–	–	1	1
59.	Malaysia	–	–	1	1
60.	Pakistan	–	–	1	1
61.	Philippines	–	–	1	1
62.	Puerto Rico	–	–	1	1
63.	Surinam	–	–	1	1
64.	Thailand	–	–	1	1

Abbreviations

ALB	Albania
ALG	Algeria
AND	Andorra
ANO	Netherlands Antilles
ARG	Argentina
AUS	Australia
AUT	Austria
BEL	Belgium
BER	Bermuda
BOL	Bolivia
BRA	Brazil
BUL	Bulgaria
CAN	Canada
CHI	Chile
CHN	People's Rep.of China
COL	Colombia
CUB	Cuba
CYP	Cyprus
KOR	Korea
CRC	Costa Rica
CRO	Croatia
DEN	Denmark
EUN	Unified Team
ESP	Spain
EST	Estonia
ETH	Ethiopia
USA	United States of America
FIN	Finland
FRA	France
GER	Germany
GBR	Great Britain
GRE	Greece
HON	Honduras
HUN	Hungary
IND	India
IOP	Independent Olympic Participant
IRI	Islamic Republic Iran
IRL	Ireland
ISL	Iceland
ISV	Virgin Islands
ITA	Italy
JAM	Jamaica
JPN	Japan
LAT	Latvia
LIB	Lebanon
LIE	Liechtenstein
LIT	Lithuania
LUX	Luxembourg
MAR	Morocco
MEX	Mexico
MON	Monaco
MGL	Mongolia
NOR	Norway
NZL	New Zealand
NED	Netherlands
PHI	Philippines
POL	Poland
PUR	Puerto Rico
PRK	Democratic People's Rep. of Korea
ROM	Romania
RSA	Republic South Africa
SMR	San Marino
SEN	Senegal
SLO	Slovenia
SWE	Sweden
SUI	Switzerland
SWZ	Swaziland
TPE	Chinese Taipei
TCH	Czech and Slovak Federative Republic
TUR	Turkey
VEN	Venezuela
YUG	Yugoslavia

Above: Corrida da toros, Spain's national sport. One man against specially-bred bulls, this type of ritual fight usually ends with the death of the bull.

The phoenix rises

The Olympic Games programme extended over a fortnight and it gave spectators, athletes and officials a chance to savour the atmosphere of the host city, to sample its cultural heritage and to meet its people. But any visitor would find it an enchanting and captivating place.

Climate and location have played a major part in drawing people from all over Spain and beyond, providing a stimulating and enriching an environment. Barcelona also enjoys a broad cultural heritage stretching back over the centuries, as George Orwell found when he visited the city 55 years ago under very different circumstances. He was there, along with many other idealistic British men and women, fighting vainly against the Fascist army of General Franco. The once opulent Catalan capital had become a grimy Mediterranean port. In the repressive Franco years that followed, industrial development turned Barcelona into an ugly, polluted conurbation. Any creative spirit was snuffed out by Franco's henchmen. In the years before it had been a liberal, creative and cultured city. At the turn of the century, architects, such as Antonio Gaudí had created a unique atmosphere. The work of artists, such as Picasso, Miró and Tàpíes, left lasting images in the people's minds. But dust and decay settled on these reminders of a time when Barcelona attracted international acclaim. Franco's death in 1975 gave the Catalans their freedom back and then, 11 years later, the vote of the Olympic Committee gave them the means with which to make a fresh start. The renovation of the historic old town, the construction of 30 miles of ring roads, the new airport and a motorway linking airport to city – all this was possible, because very large amounts of money were put into the city's coffers very quickly. No Olympic host has undertaken so much construction. No Olympic host has offered such tempting distractions. The operation was colossal, hugely successful and it has brought Barcelona and Spain lasting benefits.

Left: Special effects.
Lights play on
the fountain in front
of the Palacio
Nacional.

Above: Passeig de Colom.
Impressive columns line this busy
boulevard, which leads to
the Christopher Columbus Monument.

Above: The Montjuic stadium,
built in neo-classical style in 1929,
overlooks Barcelona's port. It was re-built
for the 1992 Games.

A world united

A thousand lights sparkled in the Catalan night, as Beethoven's 'Ode to Joy' rang out. Gun salutes and fireworks brought to an end a breathtaking three-hour spectacle watched in the stadium by 65,000 and by at least two billion at home on their television. The Spanish hosts for the XXV Olympiad presented all of them with a magnificent show, and it wasn't just a firework display. This performance eclipsed all other ceremonies, with a skilful mix of surrealistic dreamland and pure theatre. Sport and culture embraced each other on the Olympic stage. Spanish celebrities, such as the tenor José Carreras, who had directed the music, sang the Olympic hymn with such emotion that a collective frisson shimmered round the stadium like a Mexican wave.

It was a night for unity. The ceremony had begun with 600 dancers in white, accompanied by the soprano, Montserrat Caballé and José Carreras. Then came 300 drums of Aragon, the Flamenco dancers from Andalusia and the voyage of Hercules to the haunting music of Japanese composer Ryuichi Sakamoto. The human pyramids, constructed with around 2,200 gymnasts, served as a reminder to the world that co-operation and brotherhood can be stronger than any obstacles to peace. The word 'Hola' (welcome) was created from human flesh and blood and the same message resounded from the stands to the young visitors from all over the world. The enthusiastic Spanish hosts did their best to ensure that the opening ceremony, was not just some sterile ritual.

The athletes parade was led by Greece, traditionally the first team in the procesion. Next came the South African team, with Jan Tau, the black marathon runner, bearing their flag. Nelson Mandela was present with 20 heads of state and had travelled to the ceremony by coach with Samaranch. Every one of the 173 national Olympic committees was there, except the former Yugoslavia.

As the parade progressed, there were many who could not restrain their feelings. The sister of Crown

Taking aim. The arrow that set the games alight about to leave the bow of archer Rebollo.

The labours of Hercules (right). Hydra, the water-monster with many heads attacks Hercules' ship.

Prince Felipe, who was the flag-bearer for the Spanish team and a member of the Spanish yachting team, was moved to tears.

For athletes from the Ivory Coast with their cameras around their necks, Coubertin's Olympic motto, 'the important thing is to take part' was anything but a tired old cliché. Even the fêted professionals were overcome by the special atmosphere of this occasion. Wimbledon winners, Steffi Graf and Michael Stich, were in agreement: "It was simply phenomenal. There is no comparison – to be with all the athletes in the stadium". Modern gladiators and pure amateurs, gum-chewing American basketball millionaires and swaggering strongmen from Mongolia gave the world a unique demonstration of brotherhood. The climax of the opening ceremony came when a handicapped archer fired an arrow that streaked across the darkened Montjuic stadium, high above the city, to light the flame that would burn until the closing ceremony on August 9. But the most symbolic moment of all came just before the close. In darkness, a line of couriers ran between the massed ranks of the competitors. Floodlights suddenly bathed the arena, as a 6,000 square-metre Olympic flag spread outwards above the heads of the 12,000 athletes and officials. The ceremony closed to the voices of Domingo, Carreras, Caballé, Pons, Aragall and an unknown boy-treble silhouetted against the sky. Verdi's 'Triumphal March' from Aida filled the humid night.

Queen of the Flamenco dancers, Christina Hoyos enters on horseback (below). Fiery footwork on stage (left).

One of the sun-children (below). A colourful display performed in Barcelona´s scorching heat.

A flag for the world. Raising the Olympic flag with its five rings, one for each continent (above).

Elegant headgear for Boris Becker (above). Former Wimbledon champion enjoying himself with his German team-mates.

27

MEN'S SPRINT

It was my day

The streak of lightning from London ran the race of his life: Linford Christie won the gold in the 100 metres (right).

Christie overcame the weight of his years and broke the dominance of the Americans, who had to manage without Carl Lewis.

This time, the one-time king of the sprint track was not in on the game. But as the eight dark-skinned men bent down over the starting blocks, the war of nerves had long since begun. One European and the rest of the world had gathered to take over the title of the great Carl Lewis in the 100 metre sprint. Even in slow motion afterwards, it was impossible to say with any certainty which muscle-bound body had been the first off the blocks. Nevertheless, Leroy Burrell was flagged down for a false start. That was enough to set the nerves of this US star on edge, a man who had shocked all the competitors in the semi-finals by the ease with which he ran the fastest time.

Mitchell and Burrell were favourites

But, the winner is the one with nobody beside him in on the finishing line. None could say this with greater assurance than Burrell's compatriot, Dennis Mitchell, whose victory in the American trials had finally propelled him on to a far wider sporting stage. It was his upraised arm that had led to the second attempt to start the race being abandoned. His intention had merely been to signal to his competitors the new-found confidence of this one-time underdog. But after the actual race had begun, all eyes were upon the Nigerian Adeniken and the two American favourites.

Race against time

Meanwhile, almost imperceptibly, one sprinter was making headway in the centre lane. This unexpected burst by Linford Christie for the gold medal has been a race against time. At 32 years three months, he is the oldest man to win what must be the Olympic's 'blue riband' race. "Their chance will come again," Christie told an army of perspiring interrogators after the race, referring to the younger men whose hopes were dashed by his powerful performance. Christie did it through self-belief and the power of concentration. It was 20 years ago in Munich that Valery Borzov

Entering a new dimension
with Kevin Young (above and top):
the American set a remarkable
new world record over the
400 m hurdles.

4 x 100 m: Carl Lewis appears
to be losing his heart to three lightning fast men. The quartet
from the USA broke the world record.

Linford Christie
a slumbering giant

won the same race more or less unchallenged from the start.

Well-judged start

In fact, it was an anti-climax to think that nothing much happened on the way to the line. Christie's start was well-judged and he picked up through to 25 metres and from there to the line he led, with those around him fading, while he motored home on full throttle. The Olympic 100 metres lasts seconds, but it is ten seconds that can grant wealth and recognition to last a life time.

Misspent youth

Stories of Linford's misspent youth are legion. At 25, he was an athletic layabout, preferring partying to work-outs on damp, cold nights in West London within sight of Wormwood Scrubs. He needed careful handling, but Ron Roddan, his coach and Andy Norman, the British promotions officer succeeded in motivating him. They recognised that here was a slumbering giant and Roddan, in particular, deserves credit for Christie's triumph. The age of 25 is very late to start working on any Olympic event, but slowly and erratically, the work produced results. There were times when he attracted tabloid headlines. The incident in Seoul, where he was accused of taking a banned substance, threatened his career, but he was cleared.
The name of Carl Lewis was bound, sooner or later, to emerge in the aftermath. Lewis was suffering the effects of a virus, had failed to

qualify and did not run, but as Christie said: "He wasn't there on the day. It was my day."

A great way to go

In the aftermath of one of the finest 400 metres hurdle races ever run, Kriss Akabusi lingered on the Montjuïc stadium track with hands on hips to watch the re-run on the giant television screen. As Kevin Young of the United States strode through to the gold medal in a new record world time of 46.77 seconds. Akabusi could only smile and shake his head disbelievingly.
His part in the final had been memorable - a British record time of 47.82 which brought him a bronze medal behind Winthrop Graham of Jamaica. For Akabusi, these were to be his final Games, his last major championship, but it was a fine way to go. "It was a great way to end a career. This is the Olympic Games. I can't finish anywhere better. I've finished at the top. I have stood on three medal podiums at the last three major championships." The former Army sergeant received tremendous support from the British fans in Barcelona and Kriss paid tribute to the warmth of their encouragement. "Without them it would have been so much harder." But he also paid tribute to the gold medallist, who had put paid to his own hopes of taking the top spot on the podium. "I thought I was running fast, but when this guy came flying past me, then I thought 'this guy means business'." And so he did. Young powered into the back straight leaving Akabusi to

Success eluded him: Leroy Burrell (above left) gave it his all and yet failed to get a medal.

The succession: Ben Johnson tried to relive old times (centre left) but was eliminated in the semi-finals.

Injured. Mark Witherspoon's bad luck became Carl Lewis' good luck - a place in the victorious relay team.

Kenya against the rest

Dieter Baumann (below and far right) beat the strong African contingent in the 5000 metres. In the 3000 metres steeplechase, Kenyan runners took gold, silver and bronze. The Moroccan, Khalid Skah (right), won the 1000 metres, but there was an inquiry after an alleged incident with a fellow countryman.

fight out the silver and bronze position. Although Winthrop Graham hit the final hurdle, he managed, not only to maintain his balance, but also keep his narrow lead over Akabusi.

Thwarted by the wind

Life punishes the latecomers, and there are no exceptions to this rule not even for a newly-crowned Olympic champion. At least Linford Christie was in good company when he failed to qualify in the semi-final of the 200 metres. The clear favourite, Michael Johnson, did not make it either. The mantle of favourite then passed to Mike Marsh, also from the U.S.A., who ran a fantastic 19.73 seconds into a headwind in the semi-final, failing to beat Pietro Mennea's long-standing world record by a mere one hundredth of a second. So a new record seemed on the cards in the final. Marsh stormed to victory, but his disappointment was palpable when he looked up at the scoreboard. The time, 20.01 seconds after a slow start, was not good enough for this ambitious sprinter. Second place went to overjoyed Frankie Fredericks from Namibia, who thus added a second silver to the one he won in the 100 metres.

Giant strides towards success

"Allow me to present Quincy Watts, the man who is learning how to run a quarter mile." That is how the college coach, Jim Bush, used to introduce his protégé to the public a year before the Barcelona Games. The final of the 400 metres

Mike Marsh ran the second-fastest time in history in the 200 metres sprint.

400 metres is too much for a sprinter. Quincy Watt still joined the top ranks.

And everyone thought that the 1500 metres was the domain of the African runners. But olé, the Spanish runner, Fermin Cacho (right) comes home first.

left little doubt that Quincy had been a very good pupil. With his giant strides, the former basketball player left his team-mate, defending Olympic champion Steve Lewis, standing in the last 100 metres. Watts' new coach, John Smith, talked about 'Q for Quincy or Quality'. A dip in the record books shows what he meant. This gauche boy from the Chicago ghetto who had come to athletics late had run the second-fastest time ever – 43.50 seconds. The world record is held by Butch Reynolds, who was banned from competing in the Olympics after testing positive and had tried in vain to secure his passage to Barcelona through legal action. As far as Smith is concerned, it is only a matter of time before Watts breaks Reynolds' record of 43.29 seconds. "I'm convinced he will become the best 400 metres runner of all time," he said.

The race was already over as the runners turned into the finishing straight. But the last hurdle on the road to immortality was nearly his undoing. Kevin Young stumbled slightly. Had the changeover from a 12- to 13-stride pattern cost him the world record? It was an unnecessary worry. Fifteen metres before the line, he was already raising his arm in triumph. And at the finish he probably had the happiest surprise of his life. "I wanted gold and wasn't bothered about the world record, but I'll take both," was his first reaction. With 46.78 seconds, the 25-year-old sociology student from Los Angeles had shattered the old record held by the legendary Ed Moses (who had still beaten him to the bronze medal in Seoul). Young became the first man to run the 400 metres hurdles in under 47 seconds. The great Moses had missed it by two hundredths of a second when he set his record nine years previously. "I suppose I did think of the record," Young admitted afterwards. The proof was in his small room in the Olympic village, which he shared with Quincy Watts. On the wall he had taped a small note with 46.89 on it. "You have to set yourself ambitious targets," Young explained with a roguish but ever-so-contented smile. How many people can claim that they made apparently reckless predictions come true?

When there are world records to be celebrated, Carl Lewis is never far away. Either applauding on the sidelines, or as a competitor in the track – the man has a showman's touch. "I dedicate this victory to Mark Winterspoon," said the superstar, blinking ingenuously into the television camera. The great Carl had good reason to be grateful. It was an injury to his team-mate which gave him the chance to lead the US 4 x100 metres relay team to victory and win his eighth Olympic gold medal. "This is the best relay team in history," he declared. And who could disagree with him after it set a new world record of 37.40 seconds?

Another bronze for Britain

The extraordinary efforts of the men's 4 x 400 relay team managed to bag yet another bronze medal for Britain in the very closing stages of the Olympics. The team

The Kenyans, Nixon Kiprotic and William Tanui dominated the 800 metres.

led off with Roger Black, a member of the gold-winning 400m relay team at the 1991 World Championships. Black had been disappointing in his own event, the 400 metre sprint, but no one could blame him for not measuring up to the extraordinarily powerful opposition being put up in the relay by the Americans. The performance of the American team was so outstanding that it resulted in an almost embarrassing runaway. On the British side, 19 year-old Dave Grindley ran an inspired second leg. But neither Kriss Akabussi, the bronze medallist in the 400 metres hurdles nor John Regis could make any impression on the Americans this time.

Cheated of victory

An official on the track trying to push aside a lapped runner, elbows flying around the final bend, and loud jeering at the finish. These were ugly scenes not easily forgotten. On day four of the athletics competition, the Olympic Games had an almighty scandal on its hands. In the men's 10,000 metres final, the Kenyan Richard Chelimo

Andrei Perlov celebrates as he crosses the line in the 50 kilometre walk.

apparently seemed to become the innocent victim of a Moroccan plot. Khalid Skah, the eventual winner, and his lapped countryman Hammou Boutayeb, seemed to impede the Kenyan as he tried to step up the pace. The Kenyans lodged a protest and Skah was disqualified. But the International Amateur Athletics Federation (IAAF) accepted an appeal by the Moroccan Association, and so the gold medal returned once again to Skah. He was happy to play the innocent: "When Boutayeb joined us I told him to get out if the way, but he did not understand me."

The Kenyan officials could not understand the questionable decision by the IAAF. They threatened to walk out, but in the end everyone must have been grateful that they did not, because the runners from the East African plateau achieved a surprising double success in the 800 metres and an impressive clean sweep in the 3,000 metres steeplechase. At the medal ceremony the shield-and-spears flag of Kenya hung from all three poles.

A family affair

Derek Redmond from Towcester in Northamptonshire should have won a medal in the 400 metres. The experts thought that he ought at least to have made it to the finals. He started well in the semi-finals – then it looked as though he had been struck by a bullet. Suddenly, he stumbled, fell, got up, hopped one step further, his face couldn't hide the pain. He had pulled a muscle. Four years earlier in Seoul, only minutes before the start of the race, he had torn his Achilles tendon. Now he was limping along the track, while the other athletes fought it out to the bitter end. Urged on by the will to win, he had overstepped the mark. After eight years of training, something inside told him to drive himself that bit harder, to make that final, desperate push for home.

On the other side of the stadium below the Olympic flame, the figure of an old man in a pair of shorts and a hat could be seen climbing over the barrier. He crossed the track - none of the officials tried to stop him. The man easily caught up with his son. He supported him, wiped away the tears, led him round the track and over the finishing line. Nobody would have dared to stop him. There are plenty such stories surrounding the Olympic Games. Later it emerged that Derek and his father Jim had agreed that, whatever happened, he would make it to the end. That is the story of Derek Redmond, whose name did not appear on the Olympic roll of honour.

What? That wasn't a world
record? Mike Conley can't believe
it. The back wind was too strong.

Javier Sotomayor dedicated
his high jump victory to the Cuban
people.

Third Olympic gold for
Carl Lewis - a truly spectacular
athlete

Carl Lewis described world-record
holder Mike Powell as the
best opponent he'd ever had.

The battle of the titans and a fall from grace

The much-heralded 'festival of nine metre jumps' never materialised. Instead, it was pretty much business as usual, with Carl leading and Mike not far behind. Such is often the extent of any tactical play in long jumps. Carl Lewis was forced to look on helplessly as his opponent tried to better his final jump. Lewis, six times an Olympic champion, was left hoping, fearing and praying. Mike Powell was reduced to similar humility: with shaven head and hands folded, the world champion was left to wait upon the judgement of the score board. "I thought the last jump had been sufficient," Powell said of the jump which won him the silver medal. "Less than optimal," Lewis had said of his own first jump, which was nevertheless 'sufficient' to gain him the gold medal in this discipline. 8.67 m and a lead of 3 cm were enough to avoid a re-occurrence of the 'little local difficulty' in Tokyo, when Mike Powell's amazing leap of 8.95 m had robbed Lewis of the world championship, of a dream and of his reputation for invincibility. "I would like to have jumped further, but that distance was enough. That's all that counts."

One athlete was even fêted in larger-than-life size on the wall of a Barcelona house. 'Superman' Bubka - a man who has his world records decorated to order with gold medals - had come to increase his market value even further with a second Olympic title in this discipline. The plan was a simple one: 22 vaults of over six metres as proof of his superiority - what could

Sergei Bubka's supremacy in the pole-vault came to an end after three failed attempts.

The new pole-vaulting champion, Maxim Tarassov (above).

go wrong with that? "I spent far too long preparing for each jump, time was just running out on me," an overly-nervous Bubka explained afterwards. For Bubka, the 7 August 1992 will forever be remembered as 'the flop of the century' in the history of athletics. The spectators in the stadium and the millions watching on TV simply could not believe their eyes as this pole-vaulting superstar failed to achieve what for him should have been a ludicrously easy 5.70 m as a first vault. A fall from a great and lonely height, and this time an unpaid one at that.

Then there came a tableau with some rarity value. Five athletes, no less, had jumped 2.34 m. The winners' podium was becoming too crowded to hold all the high jumpers. After the Cuban world record holder and 'first among equals', Javier Sotomayor, and the Swede, Patrik Sjöberg, there was a trio of jumpers as living proof of how closely contested the Olympic standard is. Arthur Partyka from Poland, the 18 year-old Australian, Timothy Forsythe and the American, Hollis Conway were all able to gain third place and a bronze medal.

There was a lone victor. The gold medal was his for certain, but for the triple jumper, Mike Conley, it seemed no longer of much value after his 18.17 m jump. The American drummed furiously with his hands on the track in anger at an invisible opponent. A tailwind of 2.1 m/sec had prevented him from breaking the world record.

When it came to the men's shot put,

Bronze for Backley

all three medal winners had a history of previous convictions for drug-taking. But the ban on the US gold medal winner, Michael Stulce, expired four months before the start of the Games. The ban on his compatriot, Jim Doehring was only lifted shortly beforehand because of a legal technicality. And the bronze medallist, Vjatcheslav Lykho had had his gold medal in the European championships taken away for drug abuse. The first of the medal ceremonies in athletics was thus a gala of (hopefully reformed) sinners. A reputation is apparently no bar to success.

Nor is a spotless record proof against failure. Steve Backley looked like one of Britain's flagships on going into the Games, but his arrival in Barcelona was marred by disappointment. Backley always aims for a big opening throw - this was how he won his Commonwealth and European titles - but it was evident when he could only manage 82.44m on his first attempt, that all was not as it should be. Two throws earlier, the Czech, Jan Zelezny, had effectively secured the gold medal with an Olympic record throw of 89.66m, which stood as the best for the night. It was a hard act for Backley to follow. His roar of release turned into a cry of pain. as his hand went instinctively to his strapped right elbow. To compound his problems, he strained a muscle on his fourth throw, but still managed to make a marginal improvement to 83.38m, earning a bronze behind Raty of Finland, who threw 86.6m.

Britain's reigning European champion, Steve Backley will have been disappointed with the bronze. He was tipped for the title.

Despite winning the silver medal in the discus, Jürgen Schult had his disagreements with the officials.

Perfect co-ordination. Hammer-thrower Andrei Abduvaliyev (EUN) was the only one of the strong men to throw beyond the 82 metre mark.

Paul Meier (below) was the top performer on the first day in the decathlon. A worrying start for the favourite, but the fans fêted their fellow countryman.

Long, Meier and Dauth stormed out of the starting blocks (above). Dave Johnson's fourth shotput caused a stir on the first day.

A hard act to follow

The winner of the men's decathlon and the women's heptathlon could easily be described as the 'the greatest athletes in the world'. Both competitions are spread over two days and require vast reserves of speed, strength and stamina. British athletics fans do not need to be told that the name of Daley Thompson is more or less synonymous with the decathlon. A controversial character, his international career really came to an end in Seoul four years ago and he has been fighting to get fit and have one last shot at regaining the title which he won in Moscow and held on to in Los Angeles with the added bonus of breaking the world record. Thompson's decision to pull out came dramatically and painfully at Crystal Palace only weeks before the Barcelona opening. "There was a mechanical failure and that was it," he shrugged after tearing the hamstring of his right leg just before the half-way point of the opening event. That certainly was it. Asked whether this was the end, he replied: "Yes, this is where I came in".

For the decathlon, athletes have to put themselves through a gruelling two days of events ranging from the 100 metres sprint to the pole vault. The winner is established by

What would the decathlon be like without Daley Thompson, Dan O'Brien or Christian Schenk? Czech, Robert Zmelik (above) didn't mind. He had the gold medal in his sights.

Spaniard, Antonio
Penalver (above)
reaching undreamt —
of heights with his
pole-vault.
Christian Plaziat
(right) breaks free of
the blocks.

Thorsten Dauth
(right) one of the
three Germans, who
continued that
country's tradition
in the decathlon.

adding up the points in the ten events. Daley Thompson is the world record holder having amassed a total of 8,847 points in 1984. In Seoul, the East German, Christian Shenk, took the gold medal, but his points score was over 400 behind Thompson's record. The event was to miss Thompson's now slightly mellowed abrasiveness and his cheeky smile. America's Dave Johnson succeeded in taking the bronze medal for the USA, even though the Olympic judges were called in to rule over a shotput dispute. The American with the pink glasses was granted a fourth throw after his first three had been adjudged invalid. "It was disgraceful," complained the German coach, Klaus Marek. The battle for gold and silver was between the Czechoslovakian, Robert Zmelik and Antonio Penalver of Spain. Not surprisingly, the Spaniard had tremendous vocal support and many of his supporters missed out on their siestas to watch him pole vaulting through the mid-day heat. At one stage, he looked to have the gold medal within his grasp, as he equalled his best of 4.90 metres. But Zmelik went to 5.10 metres and added a few more points to his lead with a longer javelin throw. In the final event, the 1,500 metres, the gap between them gave the Czechoslovak a comfortable winning margin with a score of 8,611. He had come within 236 points of Thompson's world record. The Londoner, Dave Bigham, appearing in his first major championship, finished 18th with 7,754. Daley Thompson's sense of fun was sorely missed. "What I always enjoyed about it more than anything else is that I managed to brighten up people's lives." Maybe the Czechs had their lives brightened up, but Dave Bigham has a hard act to follow.

Zmelik and Müller
after the
1500 metres
(above).

Robert Zmelik (left)
won the decathlon
and joined the 8,000
points club. Dave
Johnson, the USA's
hope, took the bronze.

RESULTS

Marathon winner, Young-Cho Hwang of South Korea recovers from his ordeal.

Gold medal and world record for the American 4 x 400m relay team.

Kriss Akabusi looks happy. He only won the bronze, but he seems well satisfied.

100m

Men	01.08.1992
1. L. Christie (GBR)	9.96
2. F. Fredericks (NAM)	10.02
3. D. A. Mitchell (USA)	10.04
4. B. Surin (CAN)	10.09
5. L. R. Burrell (USA)	10.10
6. O. Adeniken (NGR)	10.12
7. R. D. Stewart (JAM)	10.22
8. D. Ezinwa (NGR)	10.26

200m

Men	06.08.1992
1. M. Marsh (USA)	20.01
2. F. Fredericks (NAM)	20.13
3. M. Bates (USA)	20.38
4. R. C. da Silva (BRA)	20.45
5. O. Adeniken (NGR)	20.50
6. J. P. L. Regis (GBR)	20.55

400m

Men	05.08.1992
1. Q. Watts (USA)	43.50
2. S. Lewis (USA)	44.21
3. S. Kitur (KEN)	44.24
4. I. Morris (TRI)	44.25
5. R. Hernandez Prendes (CUB)	44.52
6. D. Grindley (GBR)	44.75
7. I. Ismail (QAT)	45.10
8. S. Takano (JPN)	45.18

800m

Men	05.08.1992
1. W. Tanui (KEN)	1:43.66
2. N. Kiprotich (KEN)	1:43.70
3. J. Gray (USA)	1:43.97
4. J. L. Barbosa (BRA)	1:45.06
5. A. Benvenuti (ITA)	1:45.23
6. C. Robb (GBR)	1:45.57

1500m

Men	08.08.1992
1. F. Cacho Ruiz (ESP)	3:40.12
2. R. El-Basir (MAR)	3:40.62
3. M. A. Sulaiman (QAT)	3:40.69
4. J. Chesire (KEN)	3:41.12
5. J. Birir (KEN)	3:41.27
6. J.-P. Herold (GER)	3:41.53
7. N. Morceli (ALG)	3:41.70
8. J. Spivey (USA)	3:41.74
9. G. Hood (CAN)	3:42.55

5000m

Men	08.08.1992
1. D. Baumann (GER)	13:12.52
2. P. Bitok (KEN)	13:12.71
3. F. Bayisa (ETH)	13:13.03
4. M. B. Boutayeb (MAR)	13:13.27
5. Y. Ondieki (KEN)	13:17.50
6. W. Bikila (ETH)	13:23.52
7. R. Denmark (GBR)	13:27.76
8. A. Anton Rodrigo (ESP)	13:27.80
9. M. Issangar (MAR)	13:28.97

10 000m

Men	03.08.1992
1. K. Skah (MAR)	27:46.70
2. R. Chelimo (KEN)	27:47.72
3. A. Abebe (ETH)	28:00.07
4. S. Antibo (ITA)	28:11.39
5. A. Barrios Flores (MEX)	28:17.79
6. G. Silva Martinez (MEX)	28:20.19
7. W. Koech (KEN)	28:25.18
8. N. K. Tanui (KEN)	28:27.11
9. F. Bayisa (ETH)	28:27.68

110m hurdles

Men	03.08.1992
1. M. McKoy (CAN)	13.12
2. T. Dees (USA)	13.24
3. J. Pierce (USA)	13.26
4. T. Jarrett (GBR)	13.26
5. F. Schwarthoff (GER)	13.29
6. E. Valle (CUB)	13.41

400m hurdles

Men	06.08.1992	
1. K. Young (USA)	WR	46.78
2. W. Graham (JAM)		47.66
3. K. Akabusi (GBR)		47.82
4. S. Diagana (FRA)		48.13
5. N. Wallenlind (SWE)		48.63
6. O. Tverdokhleb (EUN)		48.63

4 x 100m relay

Men	08.08.1992	
1. USA	WR	37.40
Marsh · Burrell Mitchell · Lewis		
2. NIG		37.98
Kayode · Imoh Adeniken · Ezinwa		
3. CUB		38.00
Simon Gomez · Lamela Loaces Isasi Gonzalez · Aguilera Ruiz		
4. GBR		38.08
5. EUN		38.17
6. JPN		38.77

3000m steeplechase

Men	07.08.1992
1. M. Birir (KEN)	8:06.84
2. P. Sang (KEN)	8:09.55
3. W. Mutwol (KEN)	8:10.74
4. A. Lambruschini (ITA)	8:15.52
5. S. Brand (GER)	8:16.60
6. T. Hanlon (GBR)	8:18.14
7. B. Diemer (USA)	8:18.77
8. A. Brahmi (ALG)	8:20.71
9. W. v. Dijck (BEL)	8:22.51

4 x 400m relay

Men	08.08.1992	
1. USA	WR	2:55.74
Valmon · Watts Johnson · Lewis		
2. CUB		2:59.51
Martinez Despaigne · Herrera Ortiz Tellez · Hernandez Prendes		
3. GBR		2:59.73
Black · Grindley Akabusi · Regis		
4. BRA		3:01.61
5. NIG		3:01.71
6. ITA		3:02.18

It is to be hoped that drug-taking in the shot put event has finally been eradicated (top). In a reflective mood after the 200 metres final.

Florian Schwarthoff (above) just missed out on the bronze medal in the 110 metres hurdles.

Celebrations are in order for Daniel Plaza Montero, the Spanish gold-medal winner in the walk (above).

The 50 kilometre walkers suffered badly under the Spanish sun (above).

20km walk

Men	31.07.1992
1. D. Plaza Montero (ESP)	1:21:45
2. G. Leblanc (CAN)	1:22:25
3. G. de Benedictis (ITA)	1:23:11
4. M. Damilano (ITA)	1:23:39
5. S. Chen (CHN)	1:24:06
6. J. McDonald (IRL)	1:25:16
7. D. Garcia Cordova (MEX)	1:25:35
8. S. Urbanik (HUN)	1:26:08

50km walk

Men	07.08.1992
1. A. Perlov (EUN)	3:50:13
2. C. Mercenario (MEX)	3:52:09
3. R. Weigel (GER)	3:53:45
4. V. Spitsyn (EUN)	3:54:39
5. R. Mrazek (TCH)	3:55:21
6. H. Gauder (GER)	3:56:47
7. V. Kononen (FIN)	3:57:21
8. M. Rodriguez (MEX)	3:58:26

Marathon

Men	09.08.1992
1. Y.-C. Hwang (KOR)	2:13.23
2. K. Morishita (JPN)	2:13.45
3. S. T. Freigang (GER)	2:14.00
4. T. Nakayama (JPN)	2:14.02
5. S. Bettiol (ITA)	2:14.15
6. S. Kokaich (MAR)	2:14.25

Long jump

Men	06.08.1992
1. C. Lewis (USA)	8.67 m
2. M. Powell (USA)	8.64 m
3. J. Greene (USA)	8.34 m
4. I. Pedroso (CUB)	8.11 m
5. J. Jefferson (CUB)	8.08 m
6. K. Koukodimos (GRE)	8.04 m

Triple jump

Men	03.08.1992
1. M. Conley (USA)	18.17 m
2. C. Simkins (USA)	17.60 m
3. F. Rutherford (BAH)	17.36 m
4. L. Voloshin (EUN)	17.32 m
5. B. Wellman (BER)	17.24 m
6. Y. Quesada (CUB)	17.18 m

High jump

Men	02.08.1992
1. J. Sotomayor (CUB)	2.34
2. P. Sjöberg (SWE)	2.34
3. A. Partyka (POL)	2.34
3. T. Forsythe (AUS)	2.34
3. H. Conway (USA)	2.34
6. R. Sonn (GER)	2.31
7. T. Kemp (BAH)	2.31
8. M. Drake (CUB)	2.28

Pole vault

Men	07.08.1992
1. M. Tarassov (EUN)	5.80 m
2. I. Trandenkov (EUN)	5.80 m
3. J. Garcia (ESP)	5.75 m
3. K. Tarpenning (USA)	5.75 m
5. D. Volz (USA)	5.65 m
6. A. Peltoniemi (FIN)	5.60 m

Decathlon

Men	06.08.1992
1. R. Zmelik (TCH)	8611
2. A. Peñalver (ESP)	8412
3. D. Johnson (USA)	8309
4. D. Szabo (HUN)	8199
5. R. Muzzio (USA)	8195
6. P. Meier (GER)	8192
7. W. Motti (FRA)	8164
8. R. Ganiev (EUN)	8160
13. F. Müller (GER)	8066

Discus

Men	05.08.1992
1. R. Ubartas (LIT)	65.12 m
2. J. Schult (GER)	64.94 m
3. R. Moya (CUB)	64.12 m
4. C. Grasu (ROM)	62.86 m
5. A. Horvath (HUN)	62.82 m
6. J. Martinez (ESP)	62.64 m

Javelin

Men	08.08.1992
1. J. Zelezny (TCH)	OR 89.66 m
2. S. Raty (FIN)	86.60 m
3. S. Backley (GBR)	83.38 m
4. K. Kinnunen (FIN)	82.62 m
5. S. Einarsson (ISL)	80.34 m
6. J. Laukkanen (FIN)	79.20 m

Hammer

Men	02.08.1992
1. A. Abduvaliyev (EUN)	82.54 m
2. I. Astapkovich (EUN)	81.96 m
3. I. Nikulin (EUN)	81.38 m
4. J. Logan (USA)	79.00 m
5. T. Gecsek (HUN)	77.78 m
6. J. Tamm (EST)	77.52 m

Shot put

Men	31.07.1992
1. M. Stulce (USA)	21.70m
2. J. Doehring (USA)	20.96 m
3. V. Lykho (EUN)	20.94 m
4. W. Günthör (SUI)	20.91 m
5. U. Timmermann (GER)	20.49 m
6. K. Bodenmüller (AUT)	20.48 m

WOMEN'S SPRINT

Superb Sally

A jubilant Gwen Torrence after coming in first in the 200 metres sprint (right).

Gail Devers (right), winner of the 100 metres, made an amazing recovery after suffering from a rare glandular disorder. Merlene Ottey (below right).

Sally Gunnell is due to get married on October 19 and was hoping for a quiet time, but thanks to her superb performance in the 400 metres hurdles, which saw her become the first British woman athlete to win an Olympic gold medal since Ann Packer in 1964, this Essex girl will be the subject of intense media interest in the remaining months of the year. There was something wholesome about her moment of triumph, which was witnessed by her family and fiancé, Jon Bigg. It was going to be a struggle between Gunnell and her colourful American rival, Sandra Farmer-Patrick and Sally went out hard from the start. By doing so, she held the advantage as the runners went down the back straight. Farmer–Patrick hesitated at the seventh hurdle, which allowed Gunnell to cut back the distance. Her superior technique learned from her years as a high hurdler proved conclusive, as she turned into the home straight. By the ninth hurdle, she was edging ahead and by the tenth, she was clear by a metre. Her grimace became a grin. As she approached the line, came the realisation that she was going to arrive there first, the expression on her face turned from a grimace to a grin. As she became champion, her arm's flew up with the grace of a ballerina's. "It was the strongest and fastest I have ever felt," she said. "I knew that once I had got to the eighth hurdle level, there was no way I was going to let it slip." She had not forgotten the Tokyo experience, when she stumbled over the last two hurdles and gave the Soviet athlete Tatyana Ledovskaya the opportunity to take gold. After receiving her medal, she stood waving her bouquet. She looked as radiant as a bride. Which will take pride of place on the mantelpiece, the wedding photo or the gold medal?

Years of training went into one race lasting less than a minute. Marie-Josée Perec from France concentrates on winning the 400 metres sprint (above).

Bronze for the relay team

The British quartet in the women's 4 x 400 metres - Phyllis Smith, Sandra Douglas, Jenny Stoute and Sally Gunnell - took the bronze easily. With Gunnell isolated on the final leg and having no chance of the silver, there was an opportunity to see what an elegant runner she can be when there are no hurdles blocking her path.

Winning gold were the Unified Team, with their American rivals coming in second.

You just have to believe in yourself

She stole the gold medal, but did not return it. After all, stealing a medal by a few hundredths of a second is hardly a crime. Little in her biography suggested the outcome. Name: Gail Devers; nationality: American; age: 25 years; speciality: sprint hurdles. The outsider par excellence. "You should never give up. You can do anything if you believe in yourself," she would tell

Britain's Sally Gunnell coming home for gold in the 400 metres hurdle (left). Gail Devers (below).

us later. No one had considered her in the betting and speculation that preceded the women's 100 metres final. As five of the finalists running neck-and-neck threw themselves at the line, the experts could not believe their eyes. But the sensation was there for all to see. Not the American, Gwen Torrence, second at last year's world championships, nor the highly regarded Irina Privalova from the Unified Team, and certainly not Merlene Ottey from Jamaica had been the first to cross. The winner's time was 10:82 seconds and only six hundredths of a second separated the first five. But Gail who? They knew her name but little else about her.

"I couldn't walk, but I wanted to run," Gail Devers recalled the worst time of her life. A thyroid gland malfunction which had been treated by radiotherapy had serious side-effects. Her legs swelled up, the doctors had no answer and as late as spring 1991, were considering amputating both her feet. But slow-

ly, the medication she was taking began to work, a ray of hope after months of agony. Gail survived the ordeal and gained a new inner strength from her illness. "There are no more obstacles for a person who has gone through this. Anything is possible." A second place at the 1991 world championships in her speciality, the 100 metres hurdles, seemed to prove her point. Faith reputedly moves mountains. But not even she could have expected her surprise victory at Barcelona.

Athlete with two faces

Even her radiant smile could not hide the fact that Gwen Torrence was a bad loser. "Three women in this race were not clean." The 27-year-old was even more specific. "Two of them finished ahead of me." She meant Irene Privalova and Gail Devers. The latter's trainer, Bob Kersee, was beside himself after this accusation of drug abuse. "This is scandalous. Apart from her medi-

cation for the thyroid problem, Gail has never taken any drugs," the top coach defended his second most successful charge (after his wife Jackie Joyner Kersee). Florence could be excused for also naming Katrin Krabbe, the woman who had beaten her in both sprint distances at Tokyo. After a month of wrangling over a positive drug test, the German double world champion's voluntary decision not to take part in Barcelona proved a blessing. During the Games, new test results were published which provi-

Sandra Farmer-Patrick (USA), regarded as the favourite in the 400 metres hurdle, but only managed a silver medal.

Gail Devers won a gold in the 100 metres, but she stumbled in the hurdles.

ded further damning evidence against Krabbe and two of her team-mates.

Just how some people change

After the 200 metres final, the previously irate athlete was all sweetness and light. With her little son on her arm and the inevitable flag draped around her shoulders, Gwen Torrence exuberantly celebrated her Olympic victory. It was a magnificent run of 21.81 seconds. "I was worried that Juliet would overtake me," she admitted, referring to her main rival, Juliet Cuthbert. Previously a bit of an unknown quantity, the Jamaican athlete repeated her silver medal winning performance over the 100 metres. In doing so, she overshadowed her more prominent team mate, Merlene Ottey, who had once again turned in a disappointing run in a major championship. "I'll take the medal, although it's the wrong colour," said a tormented Ottey, taking part in what was likely to be her last Olympics.

Sensational winners

A victory for beauty and style. Not only the athletics purists enjoyed the graceful running of Marie-Josée Perec. Some 1.80 metres tall and weighing only 60 kg, the French athlete ran light-footed like a gazelle on her way to a gold in the 400 metres. Even in the finishing straight, she continued to flow along effortlessly on her long, slender legs. The time was also very good. With 48.83 seconds, the world champion approached performances previously only achieved by powerfully-built athletes like Marita Koch and Jarmila Kratochvilova.

You can't win all the time. The last hurdle on the way to her second gold medal proved Gail Devers' undoing. Inspired by her earlier victory, the American shot out of the starting blocks and was heading for even greater glory, an unprecedented double. But then it all went wrong. She ran into the last hurdle, stumbled and virtually rolled over the line in only fifth place.

The winner, at first, did not realize what she had achieved. "I thought I was third," said Paraskevi Patoulidou later. When she saw the result of her efforts on the big screen she went wild.

The 27-year-old Greek skipped along the track like a small child, unable to express her feelings in words. "I won, I won, I can't believe it. I only came here to get to the final." She became the first Greek woman athlete to win an Olympic gold medal. A rank outsider who had started running at the age of

21, she slashed her personal best by 32 hundredths of a second. Even the royals in the VIP box lost their cool. Greece's former king Constantine and his sister Queen Sofia of Spain were both in tears hugging each other. Paraskevi's weightlifter husband, was also in tears in a far corner of the stadium. Like many others around her, Paraskevi felt she was still dreaming.

Newcomers and veterans

Some dreams were shattered and others were realized in the 4 x 100m relay. The victory of the quartet from the United States was also a triumph for a grand old lady of athletics. Sixteen years after her first appearance at the Games, a housewife and mother took her leave of the Olympics with her third relay gold. "I never thought my career would last this long." Evelyn Ashford was grateful and happy. The 100 metres champion at Los Angeles, she led off in the relay this time and laid the groundwork on which Ester Jones, Carlette Guidry and Gwen Torrence capitalized in 42.11 seconds, a world best for this

year, to finish ahead of the Unified Team. No wonder the 35-year-old was in a joking mood. "Linford Christie and Carl Lewis take me as their rôle model, because I am so old and still so good." Words like this must have sounded very bitter indeed to Merlene Ottey. Set to anchor the Jamaican team - the world champions - in the relay, the 32-year-old saw Juliet Cuthbert pull up injured just before the second baton change. The silver medallist in the 100 metres was carried off the track on a stretcher. Ottey, now 32, had also lost her last chance of an Olympic medal.

Footballer turned athlete

A surprise win by an outside right on the inside lane. Four years ago, Ellen van Langen played on the

wing for a women's football team. But the 26-year-old from the Netherlands then changed career, and with some success, since earlier in the summer, she had run the fastest time this year at 800 metres. Her victory in Barcelona occurred alongside, rather than on her beloved turf, but she is unlikely to complain. Decisively, she took advantage of a gap on the inside track for a stunning finishing sprint, to which world champion Liliya Nurutdinova from the Unified Team and Cuba's Ana Fidelia Quirot had no answer. Van Langen's success in 1:55.54 was a tactical masterpiece.

Emancipation in shorts

The crescent-shaped moon shone over Barcelona when the bell rang for the last lap. Hassiba Boulmerka in the green strip of Algeria prepared to repeat her success at the world championships and win gold in the 1500 metres. Her main rivals, Tatyana Dorovshikh and Ludmilla Rogasheva from the Unified Team were running alongside her and looked strong. But on the final

Paraskevi Patoulidou from Greece benefited from Gail Devers' fall in the 100m hurdles. She went on to win gold.

Gail's fairy tale

At Seoul, Gail Devers gave the impression of being a good hurdler with a bright future ahead of her. But then she started to complain of tiredness, exhaustion, migraines, loss of vision in one eye. She lost twelve kilos in as many weeks, but she carried on training. She continued to train until she was diagnosed as having a rare complaint affecting the thyroid gland, known to the medical profession as Graves' disease. She underwent radiotherapy. Her hair started to fall out. Blood blisters formed on her skin and then burst. Special medication was prescribed but it was on the list of banned drugs. She stopped taking the drug and she resumed her demanding training schedule. She trained so much that her legs started to swell. They were soon covered with unsightly scabs. Then in March 1991, she gave up training altogether. She could scarcely walk and had to crawl around on the floor in her flat. She found another doctor, who warned her that she would have to have both legs amputated, unless she started on a different course of treatment. That was exactly 15 months before the Barcelona opening ceremony. The treatment was changed. Gail resumed her training, A new drug was prescribed which controlled the functioning of the thyroid. On 1 August, 1992, Gail won the the 100 metres at the Barcelona Olympic Games, As she stood on the podium smiling and waving and kissing her golden trophy, she looked a picture of health.

Derartu Tulu overcame many obstacles on her way to gold

The queen of the African runners emerged at Barcelona. Derartu Tulu from Ethiopia came home ahead of all her European rivals (right).

bend, Boulmerka made her move. She had a quick look back and then surged ahead. Her time of 3:55:30 was the fifth-fastest time ever. The crowd knew it had witnessed an extraordinary performance. The applause was that much more generous than usual because Boulmerka's road to success had been particularly difficult. A pioneer in an Islamic country, she had shown great determination and above all courage. Where most women wear the veil, running in shorts is nothing if not revolutionary.

We ran for Africa

Wildly cheered on by the 60,000-strong crowd, Derartu Tulu from Ethiopia and Elana Meyer from South Africa joined in a lap of honour. With her victory in the 10,000 metres, the 20-year-old Tulu had just become the first black African women to win a gold medal at the Olympic Games. Her white opponent from South Africa could not respond when she stepped up the pace in the final lap. But after the race, no one seemed too concerned about who had come first and who came second. "The government encourages women to take up sport. But tradition puts many obstacles in our way," is how Tulu explained the delayed emancipation. Meyer could also celebrate more than her silver medal. Her country had been allowed to return to the Olympic family after a ban of 32 years, for its apartheid policy. Two worlds, two races, one continent. Or as Meyer put it: "We both ran for Africa. I think we did that very well."

Victory to in the 3000 metres goes to (far left) Yelena Romanova. In the 800 metres, Ellen van Langen can't believe it (middle). Houssiba Boulmerka succeeded against the opposition of the Algerian fundamentalists (left).

Only eight seconds between them after the 26 mile marathon. Winner, Valentin Yegerova (EUN) embraces Yuko Ari-mori (JPN).

Jackie Joyner-Kersee and Heike
Drechsler competing in a
friendly atmosphere (right).
Desperation after failure in the
high jump (above).

Heike Drechsler jumping for gold in the long jump (left).

Heike Henkel (GER) said that it had been the worst competition of her life, despite winning gold in the long jump.

No hitches for the Heike's

It must have been the worst moment of her career. At 20:40 by the Montjuic stadium clock, Heike Henkel made her third attempt at jumping a height of 1.97m to stay in the competition. Her face showed how great her fear of failure had become. Her eyelids twitched nervously at the passage of the 5,000m runners, who had just started on their course. Then her concentration was broken by other athletes warming up. "Normally, I don't mind that kind of thing," she said afterwards, but then this was hardly a case of normality. For years now, she had trained to prepare for this one moment.

Heike Henkel clearing 2.02 metres to win the gold (large picture left).

First division

Since as long ago as 1984, she had joined the 'first division' of German high jumpers, at a time when the legendary Ulrike Meyfarth won her second gold medal in Los Angeles. Heike Henkel was now trying to shake off the ever-present shadow of Meyfarth. But to do so, she needed to win that gold medal. Of course, she had what it takes, having lost just one competition during the whole of the year.

Psychological barrier

The pack of 5,000m runners having passed in front of her, Henkel made her run up. As she went into the leap, fear leapt up with her. But then came the relief of pure joy on scaling that psychological barrier on her third attempt. The fact that she still had to jump 2.02m to take the gold is largely a matter for the record. In effect, Heike Henkel had

Heike Drechsler had waited a long time for the top award. At last, she had beaten JJK.

clinched it on scaling that 1.97m. They planned to go on holiday together, the new Olympic champion announced in reply to questions about her friendship with the bronze medallist. After the results of the medals were announced, the two women hugged warmly. Jackie Joyner-Kersee told reporters, "I am very pleased for Heike, it was her day and she's earned it."

At the final of the long jump, the atmosphere was equally amicable. Sporting rivalries were outweighed by the mutual respect and sympathy of the contestants. It was this fact as much as the achievements of Heike Drechsler that caused the 64,000 spectators to cheer so enthusiastically. The 27-year-old had had a long and anxious wait before her dreams came true. "Olympic gold was what I aimed for, and now I've got it," cried the student-athlete from the former East Germany when it was clear that her 7.14m was not going to be bettered. Only a few grains of sand lay between her and the 7.12m jump by the silver medallist, Inessa Kravets of the Unified Team. In her last jump, the joint favourite, Jackie Joyner-Kersee, had given it her all. Drechsler sat nervously hunched up, waiting for her rival's result. She could hardly bear to watch. Even before the result was announced, her friend came up to congratulate her. But the tension was really only released when it was official. Just as Jackie has said, "Today was Heike's day!".

.....and so it was

It seemed unlikely that Tessa Sanderson would regain the title that she won in 1984 ...and so it was. 36-year-old Tessa was in the best of spirits after she qualified for the British javelin team for a record fifth time. Before Barcelona, she was ranked 10th in the world and knew that her best days were over, so from a personal angle, Tessa will have been more than satisfied with her best throw of 63.58m and her fourth position. Her first throw was her best, but still 4.68m behind the best first throw. From then on, the die was cast and she could only watch as two Germans and a Russian fought it out for the medals. Petra Felke, Seoul's gold medallist, was asked where the future of German javelin throwing lay. Her answer came quickly: Silke Renk. Renk's first throw sailed out to a solid 67.24m and that proved to be the second longest of the competition. A medal seemed certain, though when the Russian, Natalya Shikolenko landed a spear at a seemingly impregnable 68.26m, it looked like it was going to be a silver one. But then the sensation occurred. Renk made her final throw and the spear was hurled out in a wide arc, shimmering against the night sky. It seemed to hold its flight forever, until it finally touched down a mere six centimetres beyond Shikolenko's mark. For a moment Renk stared in utter disbelief and then turned and walked back. It looked like a winning throw.......and so it was.

Silke Renk's javelin last throw could not be beaten. After the winning throw, she could hardly contain herself (top left).

No one else threw the discus as far as Maritza Marten (top left).

The top javelin throwers: Silke Renk and Karin Forkel enjoy the glory of their victory (bottom left).

No chance against the far eastern opposition. American Pamela Dukes putting the shot (left).

59

HEPTATHLON

JJK in seventh heaven.

The heptathlon is the women's decathlon. Seven events combine to produce the 'greatest woman athlete in the world.' These multi-events are spread out over two days and test speed, strength, stamina and guts. The last British success was the girl from Belfast, Mary Peters, who made a lot of friends, with her winning smile. She won the pentathlon in Munich in 1972. Then there were five events, now there are seven: the 100 metres hurdle, 200 metres, 800 metres, high jump, shotput, long jump and javelin. The scoring system is complicated and the competitors add up points to establish a winner.

Jackie Joyner-Kersee, Flo-Jo's sister-in-law, held the world record before Barcelona with a score of 7291 points. As an indication of how much she dominates the event, the Britsh record is held by Judy Simpson with a score of 6623 points.

The problem for all of the challengers to the American champion, is that Jackie Joyner-Kersee, as well as being a superb all-rounder, was also the gold medal holder in the long jump. Her huge scores in that event gave her an unassailable lead. Germany's Sabine Braun was reckoned to have a good chance, but JJK was invincible and added one more piece of precious metal to her already extensive collection. Her score was 247 points behind her world record, but still 199 points ahead of her nearest rival, Irina Belova from the Unified Team. Braun took the bronze, achieving a personal best in the high jump, but was still 196 points behind.

Jackie-Joyner Kersee jumped 1m 91 in the high jump (right).

Germany's Sabine Braun: "I wanted silver". She threw the javelin 51m 12cm. (right)

Sabine Braun jumped a personal best in the high jump - 1m 94 (right)

"I could never beat Jackie in any contest," said Sabine.

Jackie Joyner-Kersee:
"I don't underestimate anyone, but I know that I am the best."

Sabine Braun
(above, middle):
"When I think of
winning in the
Olympics, I think of
Jackie." Her time in
the 100m hurdles
was 13.25 seconds.

Jackie Joyner-Kersee
(left): "I just think of
what I've got to do"
The American girl put
the shot 14m 13

JJK -Wonderwoman
from East St Louis v
Sabine Braun from Wat-
tenscheid. In the end, it
was no contest.

RESULTS

Success for Africa. Nigeria's 4 x 400m relay team had just won the bronze medal.

Harmony in movement in the 800 metres (above). Waiting for the gun. The tension led to many false starts (right).

100m

Women	01.08.1992
1. G. Devers (USA)	10.82
2. J. Cuthbert (JAM)	10.83
3. I. Privalova (EUN)	10.84
4. G. Torrence (USA)	10.86
5. M. Ottey (JAM)	10.88
6. A. D. Nuneva (BUL)	11.10

200m

Women	06.08.1992
1. G. Torrence (USA)	21.81
2. J. Cuthbert (JAM)	22.02
3. M. Ottey (JAM)	22.09
4. I. Privalova (EUN)	22.19
5. C. Guidry (USA)	22.30
6. G. Jackson Small (JAM)	22.58

400m

Women	05.08.1992
1. M.-J. Perec (FRA)	48.83
2. O. Bryzgina (EUN)	49.05
3. X. Restrepo Gaviria (COL)	49.64
4. O. Nazarova (EUN)	49.69
5. J. Richardson-Briscoe (CAN)	49.93
6. R. Stevens (USA)	50.11

800m

Women	03.08.1992
1. E. van Langen (NED)	1:55.54
2. L. Nurutdinova (EUN)	1:55.99
3. A. F. Quirot (CUB)	1:56.80
4. I. Yevseyeva (EUN)	1:57.20
5. M. d. L. Mutola (MOZ)	1:57.49
6. E. Kovacs (ROM)	1:57.95
7. J. Clark (USA)	1:58.06
8. L. Gurina (EUN)	1:58.13

1500m

Women	08.08.1992
1. H. Boulmerka (ALG)	3:55.30
2. L. Rogacheva (EUN)	3:56.91
3. Y. Qu (CHN)	3:57.08
4. T. Dorovskikh (EUN)	3:57.92
5. L. Liu (CHN)	4:00.20
6. M. Zuñiga Dominguez (ESP)	4:00.59
7. M. Rydz (POL)	4:01.91
8. Y. Podkopayeva (EUN)	4:02.03

3000m

Women	02.08.1992
1. E. Romanova (EUN)	8:46.04
2. T. Dorovskikh (EUN)	8:46.85
3. A. F. Chalmers (CAN)	8:47.22
4. S. O'Sullivan (IRL)	8:47.41
5. P. S. Plumer (USA)	8:48.29
6. E. Kopytova (EUN)	8:49.55
7. S. Steely (USA)	8:52.67
8. Y. Murray (GBR)	8:55.85

10 000m

Women	07.08.1992
1. D. Tulu (ETH)	31:06.02
2. E. Meyer (RSA)	31:11.75
3. L. Jennings (USA)	31:19.89
4. H. Zhong (CHN)	31:21.08
5. L. McColgan (GBR)	31:26.11
6. X. Wang (CHN)	31:28.06

4 x 100m

Women	08.08.1992
1. USA	42.11
Ashford · Jones Guidry · Torrence	
2. EUN	42.16
Bogoslovskaya · Malchugina Trandenkova · Privalova	
3. NIG	42.81
Utondu · Idehen Opara Thompson · Onyali	
4. FRA	42.85
5. GER	43.12
6. AUS	43.77

100m hurdle

Women	06.08.1992
1. P. Patoulidou (GRE)	12.64
2. La Vonna Martin (USA)	12.69
3. Y. Donkova (BUL)	12.70
4. L. Tolbert (USA)	12.75
5. G. Devers (USA)	12.75
6. A. Lopez (CUB)	12.87
7. N. Kolovanova (EUN)	13.01
8. O. Adams (CUB)	13.57

4 x 400m

Women	08.08.1992
1. EUN	3:20.20
Ruzina · Dzhigalova Nazarova · Bryzgina	
2. USA	3:20.92
Kaiser · Torrence Miles · Stevens	
3. GBR	3:24.23
Smith · Douglas Stoute · Gunnell	
4. CAN	3:25.20
5. JAM	3:25.68
6. GER	3:26.37

400m hurdle

Women	05.08.1992
1. S. Gunnell (GBR)	53.23
2. S. Farmer-Patrick (USA)	53.69
3. J. Vickers (USA)	54.31
3. T. Ledovskaya (EUN)	54.31
5. V. Ordina (EUN)	54.83
5. M. Ponomareva (EUN)	54.83

Is that what it looks like? High jumper Heike Henkel on the podium with the dreamed of gold medal (above).

The victorious American team in the 4 x 100 metres relay wave the flag (above right).

Discus

Women	03.08.1992
1. M. Marten (CUB)	70.06 m
2. T. Khristova (BUL)	67.78 m
3. D. Costian (AUS)	66.24 m
4. L. Korotkevich (EUN)	65.52 m
5. O. Burova (EUN)	64.02 m
6. H. Ramos (CUB)	63.80 m

Javelin

Women	01.08.1992
1. S. Renk (GER)	68.34
2. N. Shikolenko (EUN)	68.24
3. K. Forkel (GER)	66.86
4. T. Sanderson (GBR)	63.58
5. E. Hattestad (NOR)	63.54
6. H. Rantanen (FIN)	62.34

Marathon

Women	01.08.1992
1. V. Yegorova (EUN)	2:32:41
2. Y. Arimori (JPN)	2:32:49
3. L. M. Moller (NZL)	2:33:59
4. S. Yamashita (JPN)	2:36:26
5. K. Dörre (GER)	2:36:48
6. Gyong-Ae Mun (PRK)	2:37:03
7. M. Machado (POR)	2:38:22
8. R. Burangulova (EUN)	2:38:46
9. C. S. de Reuck (RSA)	2:39:03

High Jump

Women	08.08.1992
1. H. Henkel (GER)	2.02 m
2. G. Astafri (ROM)	2.00 m
3. J. Quintero (CUB)	1.97 m
4. S. Kostadinova (BUL)	1.94 m
5. S. Kirchmann (AUT)	1.94 m
6. S. Costa (CUB)	1.94 m

Heptathlon

Women	02.08.1992
1. J. Joyner-Kersee (USA)	7 044
2. I. Belova (EUN)	6 845
3. S. Braun (GER)	6 649
4. L. Nastase (ROM)	6 619
5. S. Dimitrova (BUL)	6 464
6. P. Beer (GER)	6 434
7. B. Clarius (GER)	6 388

Shot Put

Women	07.08.1992
1. S. Kriveleva (EUN)	21.06 m
2. Z. Huang (CHN)	20.47 m
3. K. Neimke (GER)	19.78 m
4. B. Laza (CUB)	19.70 m
5. T. Zhou (CHN)	19.26 m
6. S. Mitkova (BUL)	19.23 m

10km walk

Women	03.08.1992
1. Y. Chen (CHN)	44:32
2. E. Nikolaeva (EUN)	44:33
3. C. Li (CHN)	44:41
4. S.M. Essayah (FIN)	45:08
5. Y. Cui (CHN)	45:15
6. M. Svensson (SWE)	45:17
7. A. R. Sidoti (ITA)	45:23
8. E. Saiko (EUN)	45:23
16. H.-B. Anders (GER)	46:31

Long Jump

Women	07.08.1992
1. H. Drechsler (GER)	7.14 m
2. I. Kravets (EUN)	7.12 m
3. J. Joyner-Kersee (USA)	7.07 m
4. N. Medvedeva (LIT)	6.76 m
5. M. Dulgheru (ROM)	6.71 m
6. I. Muchailova (EUN)	6.68 m

WOMEN'S SWIMMING

The competition that lacked a soul

Franziska van Almsick, the girl from Berlin, who won a silver in the 200m freestyle.

The American, Nicole Haislett beat Franziska van Almsick to the title by a hand's length.

Olympic swimming competitions have nearly always seen outstanding victories, radiant winners, whose names and faces remain in the memory. There was Kornelia Ender and Roland Matthes. Or Shane Gould and Mark Spitz, Kristin Otto, Michael Gross or Matt Biondi. And what about Barcelona '92? There were legendary achievements, gripping contests. Eight world records and innumerable national records. On each day of the competitions 10,000 spectators formed an imposing backdrop to the sun-drenched Bernat Picornell swimming stadium. And yet the competition lacked a soul. It lacked a figure, a personality, perhaps even a team or a nation which could in itself provide a positive symbol for the spirit of these Olympic swimming competitions. In Bar-

celona, swimming was presented as the heart of the Olympics. It represented the spirit of our modern age. A tight, minutely-organised programme of 31 competitions in six days, left no room for close contacts between the sporting participants and the public. The stress and self-imposed or enforced pressure to do well was too great for most of the athletes to allow themselves any distractions. The international competition was too strong for any of them to ease off a little. And there is already too much at stake for the organisers of the Olympic games for them to permit any unscripted moments.

No personal contact

The trend to perfection went so far that not even television viewers were offered the chance of personal contact. While it is natural, during the competitions themselves, for the swimmers to glide anonymously through the water, this time viewers did not even get a glimpse of their faces after the race. Where previously images of joy and disappointment touched our hearts directly, this time slow-motion and super slow-motion repeats eclipsed the only chance of personal involvement.

Even the Hungarian, Krisztina Egerszegi, did not manage to acquire much popularity, although she won her fifth Olympic gold medal. In Seoul in 1988 she had

The slim figure of Hungary's Miss Egerszegi

won the 100 and 200 metres backstroke. Then she was just 14 years old, a little girl and the youngest Olympic swimming champion of all time. Moreover she had succeeded against the swimmers of the former East Germany, who, at that time, appeared unbeatable. In Barcelona, she repeated her victories of 1988 and added to them the 400 metres medley, the hardest discipline of all. With playful ease, the delicate Hungarian left behind even the Chinese world champion Li Lin and the American joint favourite Summer Sanders – and all in 4 minutes 36.54 seconds, one of the fastest times ever to be achieved in this event. Krisztina Egerszegi is perhaps the prototype of a new generation of women swimmers which is increasingly filling the pools since the introduction of very strict drugs tests during training.

Water is her second home

The muscle-bound power-houses with the deep voices are gradually disappearing from the record lists. The new type of champion is tall and slim, almost delicate. Like Krisztina Egerszegi: height 1.72 metres, weight 54 kilograms. She is equipped with an extraordinary feel for her position in the water, which she learnt early. She was taught to swim in Budapest when she was only four years old, and since the age of ten she has considered the water to be her 'second home'. She trains in the water for 4–5 hours a day at the Spartacus SC Club in Budapest, in addition to jogging, gymnastics and weight-

training. Her cheerful temperament helps her to cope with the strains of training, and over the years her body has not changed in its proportions. While her rivals became broader during puberty, Krisztina Egerszegi has kept the slim figure which makes possible her streamlined, ideal water position and elegant style. According to her trainer Laszlo Kiss, "she is the ideal female swimmer." And in the eyes of her fellow countrymen she is much more than just Hungary's most popular sportswoman. She has become a rôle-model, not just for the country's sport-mad youth, but also a symbol for the modern Hungarian women . With her fingernails painted purple, her unusual clothes and well-styled hair, she is a trendsetter in fashion and lifestyle – many Hungarian women try to copy her appearance.

The challenge from the East

The surprise child victor in Seoul was the most successful female swimmer in Barcelona with three gold medals, and thereby gave Hungary second place in the women's international medal tables. But first place went to to China with four gold medals: Wenyi Yang (world record in the 50 metres freestyle in 24.79 seconds), Yong Zhuang (100 metres freestyle), Hong Qian (100 metres butterfly) and Li Lin (world record in the 200 metres medley in 2 minutes 11.65 seconds). The Chinese first attracted attention as world-class swimmers at the 1990 Asian Games. Only two years later, they

Dagmar Hase (top left) would have been satisfied with silver, but took the gold in the 400m freestyle.

Australia's Hayley Jane Lewis (middle left), came in second in the 800m freestyle.

The USA's Janet Evans (bottom left) makes up for disappointment in the 400 metres, by winning the 800 metres.

Cooling down before the race. The USA's Nicole Haislett went on to win gold in the 200 m freestyle.

The powerful water-sprites from the new Middle Kingdom

Nicole Haislett and Dara Torres cheer on their American team-mates to a new world record in the 400 metres relay.

Inscrutable. Xiaohong Wang (right), China's silver medallist in the 200m butterfly. Was it joy or disappointment?

A new world record. The Chinese girl, Li Lin, beat the world record for the 200 metres medley It was set in 1981.

were already number one in the world. At their first serious Olympic appearance, the Chinese took over the mantle from the disbanded East German team. A meteoric rise!.

But instead of recognition, the upstarts from the Middle Kingdom met with only world-wide mistrust. After all, their female swimmers had nothing in common with the average Chinese woman. Were they meant to be women? They were twice the height and weight of normal Chinese women, as muscular and powerful as were once the champions from East Germany and Romania. And the means by which the latter had won their medals has been well documented in the course of the political changes in their countries. Seven out of 15 women's gold medals went to China and Hungary – the only two members of the world swimming body FINA which do not allow international drugs tests outside competitions. It made little difference, when the

sprinter Yong Zhuang tried to account for her success with stories of training as a small child: "I started to swim when I was still a baby. I never cried when I was in the water. I have always liked swimming." The mistrust remained. The shadows of the drug scandals, which had shaken the sport in the preceding month, had not yet receded. No major achievement could escape the suspicion of being aided by drugs. This was also the experience of 22 year-old Dagmar Hase from Magdeburg, the only German gold medallist in the women's swimming. In an inspiring finish, Dagmar Hase beat the favourite and defending champion, Janet Evans, from the USA in the 400 metres freestyle, and won second place behind the outstanding Krisztina Egerszegi in the 200 metres backstroke.

Victory tears

But the tears, which were streaming down her face during the medal ceremony and later in a television interview, were not an expression of joy. She was giving vent to the anger and fury, the sorrow and despair of the preceding weeks, during which she considered herself and her closest friends to have been unfairly treated. Her friend and training partner, Astrid Strauss, another Olympic favourite, had been banned for taking drugs, and her trainer was under suspicion of using illegal training methods. In this context it is only natural that Dagmar Hase's Olympic victory was celebrated in low-key fashion.

For what is one to make of this backstroke specialist, who after years of training suddenly increases her personal best time over 400 metres freestyle by an unbelievable five seconds? Too much has become known about natural and unnatural ways to boost an athlete's performance for such leaps to be naively applauded as in previous years.

Franziska van Almsick A breath of fresh air

The sole exception was Franziska van Almsick, a bright 14 year-old girl from Berlin, or more precisely from Treptow, a district of former East Berlin. With youthful nonchalance and to everyone's surprise, Franziska took first the bronze in the 100 metres freestyle and then, no longer so unexpectedly, the silver medal in the 200 metres freestyle. Only a tenth of a second separated her from the Olympic champion Nicole Haislett from the USA. Moreover, as Franziska van Alm-

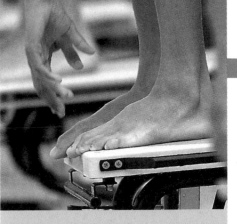

sick had herself recorded exactly the same time of 1 minute 57.90 seconds in the morning's heats, she was even a bit disappointed at taking second place, which everyone else considered a sensation. It was the third fastest time ever swum by a woman in this event, and it was done by a 14 year-old girl, albeit one who was already 1.75 metres tall. Although her trainer, Dieter Lindemann, has been criticised for his ambiguous attitude to the issue of drugs, Franziska van Almsick has been publicly acknowledged as being above all suspicion.

No more scandals

After all the scandals and revelations of the most recent past the public was yearning again for clean, unsullied sportsmen and sportswomen. Franziska van Almsick appeared just at the right time. Besides being pert, bright, open, direct and affectionate, she was successful: she attracted the support of the

public and the attention of the marketing men. She was confronted with this huge wave of popularity and its direct consequences while still in Barcelona.

Short-lived success

Franziska could also see there the associated dangers in the examples of her rivals from the USA. Setting out as clear favourites after the demise of communism in the German Democratic Republic, they already considered themselves to be number one in the world. "We can take 20 gold medals and win every race in the women's events," chief coach Mark Schubert boasted in advance. In the end, they were happy to have won three individual events (Nicole Haislett in the 200 metres freestyle; Janet Evans in the 800 metres freestyle and Summer Sanders in the 200 metres butterfly), as well as the two relays. And the three-time gold medal winner of Seoul, Janet Evans, only managed a single successful defence of her title: in the 800 metres freestyle.

Success in women's swimming has become short-lived, the era of the stars seems to be over. Only Franziska van Almsick offered a little hope for the future.

The French girl, Catherine Plewinski (left), missed out on the bronze by a fingertip in the 50 metre freestyle.

A tale of the unexpected

What's so special about sport? That's a question often asked by the committed television viewer, who is forced to miss his or her favourite programme, because of some sporting event. It cannot be easily explained, but what happened at Barcelona in one of the swimming events might go some way towards providing an answer. In the 100-metres freestyle, everybody expected the Matt Biondi to win. Four years ago in Seoul, he won five gold medals, setting a world record in the 50 metres freestyle and an Olympic record in the 100 metres freestyle. He said that he had nothing more to prove and so he set about creating a new job, that of the professional swimmer. His prospects in Barcelona were reckoned to be excellent. But what about Pablo Morales? At 27, he had plenty of experience too, having competed in Los Angeles in 1984. Two days previously, he had won the 100 metre butterfly. So, it was either Biondi or Morales - there was no one else who stood a chance. These two men, who were the fastest human beings in water, were using the Olympic swimming stadium to resolve a small, private disagreement. Biondi or Morales - that was the question. The experts gave Biondi the edge. He had the slightly better style, which might give him an advantage. The point of this story is quite simple. The gold medal for the 100 metres freestyle was won by Alexander Popov from Volgograd and a member of the United Team. That's what makes sport so special.

Spectacular swordasubs

The synchronised swimmers complain that no-one takes their sport seriously, yet it turned out to be very popular with Spanish spectators.

It has been difficult for the public to warm to synchronised swimming. It has been the butt of many jokers, but it is possible that the Barcelona Olympics may at last have brought respectability to this little understood sport. One thing is certain: synchro swimming has proved very popular with the public. For the finals of the event, tickets could only be found on the black market. It will come as a relief to the British trio, Kerry Shacklock, Laila Vakil and Natasha Haynes, who admit to being a little fed up with people making fun. "They don't realise how much work goes into it," said Kerry. "Other swimmers respect us because they know how much work goes into it." Her pre-competition schedule amounted to six hours a day of weight training, gym and pool work-outs. The British coach rejected suggestions that the synchro swimming will be cut from future Games. "It's one of the few female-only events, whereas there are lots of male-only competitions," she said. Back in the pool, one competitor performed while her team-mates got in and out of the water - all identical in black costumes and bright white caps. They performed exercises bearing exotic names such as swordasubs and barracuda back pikes. The interest of the audience never faded. At one point, there was an appeal to the spectators for silence, but it had little effect. Despite amassing a total of 179,839 points, Kerry Shacklock came seventh in the solo competition, with the gold going to the American girl Kirsten Babb-Sprague.

Karen and Sarah John
won the gold me
in the d

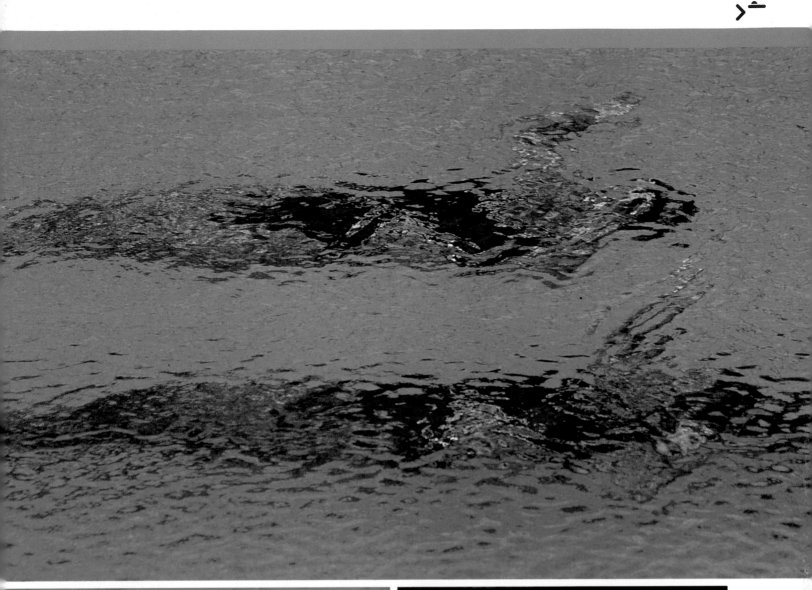

Karen and Sarah Johnson,
two American sisters, won the gold
medal and waved the stars
and stripes in celebration.

Above: Hong Qian, winner of the 100 metres butterfly. She swam as if she was being chased by a crocodile.

Two of the American swimmers in the 4 x 100m medley. Christine Ahmann-Leighton and Anita Nall celebrate.

West beats East in the 200m butterfly. The American Summer Sanders (gold) and the Chinese girl, Xiaohong Wang (silver)

50m freestyle

Women		31.07.1992
1. W. Yang (CHN)	WR	24.79
2. Y. Zhuang (CHN)		25.08
3. A. Martino (USA)		25.23
4. C. Plewinski (FRA)		25.36
5. J. Thompson (USA)		25.37
6. N. Mechtcheriakova (EUN)		25.47

100m freestyle

Women	26.07.1992
1. Y. Zhuang (CHN)	54.64
2. J. B. Thompson (USA)	54.84
3. F. van Almsick (GER)	54.94
4. N. L. Haislett (USA)	55.19
5. C. Plewinski (FRA)	55.72
6. J. Le (CHN)	55.89

200m freestyle

Women	27.07.1992
1. N. L. Haislett (USA)	1:57.90
2. F. van Almsick (GER)	1:58.00
3. K. Kielgass (GER)	1:59.67
4. C. Plewinski (FRA)	1:59.88
5. L. Dobrescu (ROM)	2:00.48
6. E. Chiba (JPN)	2:00.64

400m freestyle

Women	28.07.1992
1. D. Hase (GER)	4:07.18
2. J. Evans (USA)	4:07.37
3. H. J. Lewis (AUS)	4:11.22
4. E. M. Hansen (USA)	4:11.50
5. K. Kielgass (GER)	4:11.52
6. A. Arnould (BEL)	4:13.75
7. M. Nilsson (SWE)	4:14.10
8. S. Chiba (JPN)	4:15.71

4 x 100m freestyle

Women		28.07.1992
1. USA	WR	3:39.46
Haislett · Torres Martino · Thompson		
2. CHN		3:40.12
Zhuang · Lu Yang · Le		
3. GER		3:41.60
van Almsick · Osygus Hunger · Stellmach		
4. EUN		3:43.68
5. NED		3:43.74
6. DEN		3:47.81

100m breaststroke

Women	29.07.1992
1. E. Roudkovskaia (EUN)	1:08.00
2. A. L. Nall (USA)	1:08.17
3. S. L. Riley (AUS)	1:09.25
4. G. Cloutier (CAN)	1:09.71
5. J. Dörries (GER)	1:09.77
6. G. Csepe (HUN)	1:10.19

800m freestyle

Women	30.07.1992
1. J. Evans (USA)	8:25.52
2. H. Lewis (AUS)	8:30.34
3. J. Henke (GER)	8:30.99
4. P. Langrell (NZL)	8:35.57
5. I. Dalby (NOR)	8:37.12
6. O. Splichalova (TCH)	8:37.66

4 x 100m medley

Women		30.07.1992
1. USA	WR	4:02.54
Loveless · Nall Ahmann-Leighton · Thompson		
2. GER		4:05.19
Hase · Dörries van Almsick · Hunger		
3. EUN		4:06.44
Jivanesvskaia · Roudkovskaia Kiritchenko · Mechtcheriakova		
4. CHN		4:06.78
5. AUS		4:07.01
6. CAN		4:09.26

200m breaststroke

Women	27.07.1992
1. K. Iwasaki (JPN)	2:26.65
2. L. Lin (CHN)	2:26.85
3. A. L. Nall (USA)	2:26.89
4. E. Roudkovskaia (EUN)	2:28.47
5. G. Cloutier (CAN)	2:29.88
6. N. Giguere (CAN)	2:30.11
7. M. Dalla Valle (ITA)	2:31.21
8. A. Peczak (POL)	2:31.76

200m medley

Women		30.07.1992
1. L. Lin (CHN)	WR	2:11.65
2. S. Sanders (USA)		2:11.91
3. D. Hunger (GER)		2:13.92
4. E. Dendeberova (EUN)		2:15.47
5. E. Overton (AUS)		2:15.76
6. M. Limpert (CAN)		2:17.09

400m medley

Women	26.07.1992
1. K. Egerszegi (HUN)	4:36.54
2. L. Lin (CHN)	4:36.73
3. S. E. Sanders (USA)	4:37.58
4. H. J. Lewis (AUS)	4:43.75
5. H. Hiranaka (JPN)	4:46.24
6. D. Hunger (GER)	4:47.57

Above: A double for China in the 50m freestyle. Wenyi Yang and Yong Zhuang. Left: Dagmar Hase, German gold medal winner in the 400m freestyle.

Left: Krisztina Egerszegi, Hungary's young swimming star, collecting the gold medal from the 400m medley, just one of her three gold medals.

Three continents - three women. In the 200m medley, Asian, Lin Li won the gold, the American, Summer Sanders won the silver and the European, Daniela Hunger the bronze.

Synchronised swimming-solo

Women	06.08.1992
1. K. Babb-Sprague (USA)	191.848
2. S. Frechette (CAN)	191.717
3. F. Okuno (JPN)	187.056
4. O. Sedakova (EUN)	185.106
5. A. Capron (FRA)	182.449
6. C. Thalassinidou (GRE)	180.244

Synchronised swimming-duet

Women	07.08.1992
1. USA Josephson · Josephson	192.175
2. CAN Vilagos · Vilagos	189.394
3. JPN Okuno · Takayama	186.868
4. EUN Koslova · Sedakova	184.083
5. FRA Aeschbacher · Capron	179.366

Platform 10m

Women	27.07.1992
1. M. Fu (CHN)	461.430
2. E. Mirochina (EUN)	411.630
3. M. E. Clark (USA)	401.910
4. J. Zhu (CHN)	400.560
5. I. Afonina (EUN)	398.430
6. M. Alcala Izguerra (MEX)	394.350
12. H. J. Allen (GBR)	317.850
14. U. Wetzig (GER)	284.130

100m butterfly

Women	29.07.1992
1. H. Qian (CHN)	58.62
2. C. Ahmann-Leighton (USA)	58.74
3. C. Plewinski (FRA)	59.01
4. X. Wang (CHN)	59.10
5. S. O'Neill (AUS)	59.69
6. S. E. Sanders (USA)	59.82

200m butterfly

Women	31.07.1992
1. S. E. Sanders (USA)	2:08.67
2. X. Wang (CHN)	2:09.01
3. S. O'Neill (AUS)	2:09.03
4. M. Haruna (JPN)	2:09.88
5. R. Shito (JPN)	2:10.24
6. A. Wester Krieg (USA)	2:11.46
7. M. Jacobsen (DEN)	2:11.87
8. I. Tocchini (ITA)	2:13.78

100m backstroke

Women	28.07.1992
1. K. Egerszegi (HUN)	1:00.68
2. T. Szabo (HUN)	1:01.14
3. L. Loveless (USA)	1:01.43
4. N. Dawn Stevenson (AUS)	1:01.78
5. E. Wagstaff (USA)	1:01.81
6. J. M. Meehan (AUS)	1:02.07

200m backstroke

Women	31.07.1992
1. K. Egerszegi (HUN)	2:07.06
2. D. Hase (GER)	2:09.46
3. N. D. Stevenson (AUS)	2:10.20
4. L. E. Loveless (USA)	2:11.54
5. A. K. Simcic (NZL)	2:11.99
6. T. Szabo (HUN)	2:12.94
7. S. Poll Ahrens (CRC)	2:12.97
8. L. C. Habler (AUS)	2:13.68

Springboard 3m

Women	03.08.1992
1. M. Gao (CHN)	572.400
2. I. Lachko (EUN)	514.140
3. B. P. Baldus (GER)	503.070
4. H. Bartova (TCH)	491.490
5. J. Ovenhouse (USA)	477.840
6. V. Ilina (EUN)	470.670
7. S. Koch (GER)	468.960
8. M. K. Depiero (CAN)	449.490

A dent in the Chinese crown

Looking down on Barcelona. The amazing panorama from the top board did not affect the performance of the high divers.

For one and a half seconds, it seemed as though she would fall out of the sky directly on to Montjuic. One and a half seconds for that breathtaking dance between earth and sky: forwards, backwards, bent double, streched out or diving in a straight line - rotating in a horizontal, vertical and diagonal axis. Just by looking on you felt you were losing all sense of direction - but the young Mingxia Fu even managed to finish by entering the water with hardly a splash. None of her competitors could come close to equalling the light and lithe touch of this 1.48 metre Chinese woman; none had anything like such a pronounced feel for how to move through the air. The 13 year-old earned her Olympic gold medal. This did not, in fact, make her the youngest Olympic champion of all time. That accolade belongs to the 1936 performance of the American Marjorie Gestring. The Chinese first participated in the Olympic Games in 1984; here, in Barcelona, they had already overtaken the rest of the world, managing to win three out of four possible gold medals. Only the 24 year-old American Mark Lenzi managed to overcome this Chinese dominance. In 1991 Lenzi, a psychology graduate, was the first diver ever to have achieved more than 100 points for a single dive. This was not a performance that he managed to repeat in Barcelona's Piscina Municipal. Nevertheless, his calm and relaxed approach helped him to stem the onrushing tide of Chinese victories.

Top marks for starting position and entry. Mark Lenzi (USA) took the gold medal in the diving and the favourites went under (right and extreme right).

Mingxia Fu (left) likes listening to Madonna. Brita Baldus' (below) musical tastes are not known, but Mingxia won the gold and Brita the bronze.

Shuwei Sun (left) won the platform diving. A rather undignified Albin Killat leaves the diving pool

The water polo
tournament was a big
success in Barcelona.
The Spanish team won
the silver medal, losing
to Italy in the final.

Conspicuous even in their absence

The long shadow of the war in Yugoslavia fell over the Bernat Picornell pool, on the the very last day of the Games during the course of the penultimate event. For although Yugoslavia, the Seoul gold medallists and world and European champions, had been excluded from these Games just before the opening ceremony, battle was nevertheless joined at the water's edge between two coaches from the former Yugoslavia. Ratko Rudic, the coach for the Italian side and Dragan Matuinovic for the Spanish.

The one is a Serb, the other a Croat. A gold medal was at stake, and 9,000 spectators looked on as the Spanish favourites fought it out with the Italians in the longest and probably the most exciting play off in the history of water polo. The score was 7:7 after the standard 28 minutes of play, then 8:8 after the second extension of play. Three further extensions of play could do nothing to alter this. As the tension became ever more extreme, the two coaches set on each other in a fist fight, so that play had to be

interrupted. Eventually, the Italian Ferdinando Gandolfi brought the contest to a close. After almost an hour and a half of play, Gandolfi managed to score the decisive goal 30 seconds before the end of the sixth extension of time. Italy thus became Olympic champions for the third time after their victories in 1948 and 1960 ,and for Spain it was only the second ever Olympic medal in this discipline. The Americans, as the other favourites after winning the silver in 1984 and 1988, ended in only fourth place.

Ferezzi and Gomez struggle for the ball. Many offences are committed under-water, making the referee's job a difficult one.

The Italian team celebrating after the final. Three periods of extra-time were required to establish the winner (above).

MEN'S SWIMMING

American swimming supremacy challenged

The biggest names in swimming have usually been American names - Mark Spitz and Shane Gould are two names that readily spring to mind in the men's section. Biondi, Morales and Barrowman were expected to extend this tradition The Star Spangled Banner was heard, but not always on the occasions that the pundits had predicted. In the 100 metres breaststroke, for example, it was Nelson Diebel who mounted the winners rostrum at the expense of Britain's Nick Gillingham and Adrian Moorhouse. It was in the 100 metres freestyle that the biggest shock occurred. Matt Biondi who collected five medals in Seoul, could only manage fifth place, having failed to make any impact in the heats. Alexander Popov of the Unified Team led the cavalry charge for the line, just beating Brazil's Gustavo Borges. The South American was only awarded the silver after television evidence showed that he had failed to hit the pressure pad with enough force. He was found in the practice pool in tears and given the good news. In the 100 metres butterfly, Pablo Morales gave the US squad a fright, when it looked as if he was going to throw away a substantial lead. He managed to hold off the Pole, Rafal Szukala. The same race saw one of Seoul's swimming sensations in action. Anthony Nesty, Surinam's only Olympic gold medallist, won the bronze and then promptly announced his retirement.

Bronze for UK's Nick Gillingham

Only Mike Barrowman gave the American team a lift. The possessor of one of swimming's most awesome records, amazingly he improved on it by half a second in the 200 metres breaststroke.

Up against that sort of performance, Nick Gillingham, Britain's only medal winner in the swimming events, summoned up the race of his life.and could draw complete satisfaction from finishing third in the Bernat Piconell pool. Despite fears of a recurring thigh injury, which was threatening to turn his Games into a disaster, the silver medallist from Seoul produced a lifetime's best. Having taken an anti-inflammatory pill to blank out the pain, he swam 2min 11.29 sec-

Evgueni Sadovyi sets off as the first leg in the 4 x 200m freestyle The shaven-headed Russian won three gold medals for the Unified Team (left).

One of the French swimmers in the 4 x 100m medley. The French team came in fourth,

Nelson Diebel jumps for joy. The American had just won the 100m breaststroke. His joy became tears of emotion on the medals podium.

onds under severe mental and physical pressure. Gillingham can console himself with the fact that he had swum the fourth fastest time the world has known. He must owe his success to pure determination. "I wanted to win so much that during the race, I never felt anything," said Gillingham afterwards. "I've had about 16 hours of treatment since Sunday. My race preparation went completely out of the window." For four days, the nation had focused its interest on Gillingham's physical state His mental state was certainly

not helped by the knowledge that the silver medal winner, Hungarian, Norbert Rozsa, squeezed past him in the last 15 metres and recorded a time which was a mere six one-hundredths of a second faster. If Gillingham had suffered a crisis of confidence, he hid it well.

Making world records gets harder and harder, but one of the most impressive performances in the pool came from Evgueni Sadovyi of the United Team. He won the 400 metres freestyle in 3min 45.00 seconds to knock almost one and a

half seconds.off the world record. He really had the Swede, Anders Holmertz, to thank. The latter set a ferocious pace for the first seven lengths and was caught only at the final turn.

A look back and a look forward.

Frustrated, disappointed but not disillusioned - that was how Terry Dennison, Britain's coach summed up his feelings, after his squad had produced an uninspiring performance. The officials claimed the team, which had won only one medal, were well-prepared and optimistic. The optimism had stemmed from the euphoria of the Olympic trials in Sheffield last May, but, in the end, the swimmers found it difficult to lift themselves to their best. "To be top dog in your own country and then come here and be a nothing is difficult.," said the team psychologist Richard Cox.

They were reluctant to make excuses but British swimmers do not have the financial incentives of other countries. Australian Olympic swimmers can earn in excess of £50,000 and the top ones far more. Britain had spent between £75,000 and £100,000 on three training sessions, but this was insignificant compared to what other countries had invested.

But there are rays of hope on the horizon. A Sunderland student, by the name of Ian Wilson, came a commendable fifth in the 1500 metres. freestyle. The 21-year old lived up to expectations, but to be competing in the same race as the Australian, Kieran Perkins, took the gloss off Wilson's good performance. Perkins broke his own world record by nearly five seconds. Sadly, Wilson was half a pool adrift. Another name for the future is Paul Parker. He set a national record in the 200 metres freestyle and finished 10th fastest in the in the 400 metres heats. Another domestic record was broken by the 4 x 100 metres relay team, comprising Mike Fibbens, Mark Foster, Paul Howe and Roland Lee.

Left: Surinam's Anthony Nesty came third in the 100m butterfly. He announced his retirement immediately afterwards.

Far left: Australian, Kieren Perkins was only warming up in the 400m freestyle. In the 1500m he set a new world record.

Tamas Darnyi from Hungary, world record holder in the 400m medley, continued his successful run.

Martin Lopez-Zubero won Spain's first gold medal in the 200m backstroke.

RESULTS

An Australian double in the 1500m freestyle. The gold went to Kieren Perkins and the silver to Glen Housman. Jörg Hoffman came third but looks none too pleased about it.

Canadian Mark Tewkesbury (above) likes the taste of gold. He won the 100m backstroke.

Above: Martin Lopez-Zubero only came fourth in the 100m backstroke, but is pleased enough to want to wave the Spanish flag for his supporters.

Alexander Popov (above, middle), winner of the 50m freestyle, teams up with his American rivals, Tom Jager and Matt Biondi.

50m freestyle

Men	30.07.1992
1. A. Popov (EUN)	21.91
2. M. Biondi (USA)	22.09
3. T. Jager (USA)	22.30
4. P. Williams (RSA)	22.50
4. C. Kalfayan (FRA)	22.50
6. M. Foster (GBR)	22.52

100m freestyle

Men	28.07.1992
1. A. Popov (EUN)	49.02
2. G. Borges (BRA)	49.43
3. S. Caron (FRA)	49.50
4. J. C. Olsen (USA)	49.51
5. M. N. Biondi (USA)	49.53
6. T. Werner (SWE)	49.63

200m freestyle

Men	26.07.1992
1. E. Sadovyi (EUN)	1:46.70
2. A. Holmertz (SWE)	1:46.86
3. A. Kasvio (FIN)	1:47.63
4. A. Wojdat (POL)	1:48.24
5. V. Pychnenko (EUN)	1:48.32
6. J. B. Hudepohl (USA)	1:48.36

400m freestyle

Men	29.07.1992
1. E. Sadovyi (EUN)	WR 3:45.00
2. K. J. Perkins (AUS)	3:45.16
3. A. Holmertz (SWE)	3:46.77
4. A. Wojdat (POL)	3:48.10
5. I. R. Brown (AUS)	3:48.79
6. S. Wiese (GER)	3:49.06
7. S. Pfeiffer (GER)	3:49.75
8. D. J. Loader (NZL)	3:49.97

4 x 100m freestyle

Men	29.07.1992
1. USA	3:16.74
Hudepohl · Biondi Jager · Olsen	
2. EUN	3:17.56
Khnykine · Prigoda Bashkatov · Popov	
3. GER	3:17.90
Tröger · Richter Zesner · Pinger	
4. FRA	3:19.16
5. SWE	3:20.10
6. BRA	3:20.99

100m breaststroke

Men	26.07.1992
1. N. W. Diebel (USA)	1:01.50
2. N. Rozsa (HUN)	1:01.68
3. P. J. Rogers (AUS)	1:01.76
4. A. Hayashi (JPN)	1:01.86
5. V. Ivanov (EUN)	1:01.87
6. D. Volkov (EUN)	1:02.07

1500m freestyle

Men	31.07.1992
1. K. J. Perkins (AUS)	WR 14:43.48
2. G. C. Housman (AUS)	14:55.29
3. J. Hoffmann (GER)	15:02.29
4. S. Pfeiffer (GER)	15:04.28
5. I. Wilson (GBR)	15:13.35
6. I. Majcen (SLO)	15:19.12

4 x 200m freestyle

Men	27.07.1992
1. EUN	WR 7:11.95
Lepikov · Pychnenko Tajanovitch · Sadovyi	
2. SWE	7:15.51
Wallin · Holmertz Werner · Frolander	
3. USA	7:16.23
Hudepohl · Stewart Olsen · Gjertsen	
4. GER	7:16.58
5. ITA	7:18.10
6. GBR	7:22.57

200m breaststroke

Men	29.07.1992
1. M. Barrowman (USA)	WR 2:10.16
2. N. Rozsa (HUN)	2:11.23
3. N. Gillingham (GBR)	2:11.29
4. S. Lopez Miro (ESP)	2:13.29
5. K. Guttler (HUN)	2:13.32
6. P. J. Rogers (AUS)	2:13.59
7. K. Watanabe (JPN)	2:14.70
8. A. Hayashi (JPN)	2:15.11

200m medley

Men	31.07.1992
1. T. Darnyi (HUN)	2:00.76
2. G. S. Burgess (USA)	2:00.97
3. A. Czene (HUN)	2:01.00
4. J. N. Sievinen (FIN)	2:01.28
5. C. Gessner (GER)	2:01.97
6. R. D. Karnaugh (USA)	2:02.18

400m medley

Men	27.07.1992
1. T. Darnyi (HUN)	4:14.23
2. E. Namesnik (USA)	4:15.57
3. L. Sacchi (ITA)	4:16.34
4. D. Wharton (USA)	4:17.26
5. C. Gessner (GER)	4:17.88
6. P. Kühl (GER)	4:19.66

Mike Barrowman (left) heads home in the 200m breaststroke to set a new world record.

Bronze medallists. Franck Esposito (above) of France came third in the 200m butterfly and Britain's Nick Gillingham (left) was unlucky not to pick up the silver in the 200m breaststroke.

Fisher of men: The victorious Unified Team in the 200m relay pull Evgueni Sadovyi out of the water (above).

Winning smiles: (from the left) Alexander Popov (EUN), Stephan Caron (France) and Gustavo Borges (Brazil), the three medallists in the 100m freestyle.

Water polo

Men	09.08.1992
1. ITA	
2. ESP	
Italy — Spain	a.e.t. 9:8
3. EUN	
4. USA	
EUN — USA	8:4
5. AUS	

DIVING

Platform

Men	04.08.1992
1. S. Sun (CHN)	677.310
2. S. R. Donie (USA)	633.630
3. N. Xiong (CHN)	600.150
4. J. Hempel (GER)	574.170
5. B. Morgan (GBR)	568.590
6. D. Saoutine (EUN)	565.950
7. M. Kühne (GER)	558.540
8. K. Vaneto (JPN)	529.140

Springboard

Men	29.07.1992
1. M. E. Lenzi (USA)	676.530
2. L. Tan (CHN)	645.570
3. D. Saoutine (EUN)	627.780
4. M. A. Murphy (AUS)	611.970
5. K. M. Ferguson (USA)	609.120
6. J. Mondrag. Vazquez (MEX)	604.140
10. A. Killat (GER)	556.350
11. M. Rourke (CAN)	540.660

100m backstroke

Men	30.07.1992
1. M. Tewksbury (CAN)	53.98
2. J. Rouse (USA)	54.04
3. D. Berkopf (USA)	54.78
4. M. Lopez-Zubero (ESP)	54.96
5. V. Selkov (EUN)	55.49
6. F. Schott (FRA)	55.72
7. R. Falcon Carrera (CUB)	55.76
8. D. Richter (GER)	56.26

200m backstroke

Men	28.07.1992
1. M. Lopez-Zubero (ESP)	1:58.47
2. V. Selkov (EUN)	1:58.87
3. S. Battistelli (ITA)	1:59.40
4. H. Itoi (JAP)	1:59.52
5. T. Schwenk (USA)	1:59.73
6. T. Weber (GER)	1:59.78
7. T. Deutsch (HUN)	2:00.06
8. S. Maene (BEL)	2:00.91

100m medley

Men	27.07.1992
1. P. Morales (USA)	53.32
2. R. Szukala (POL)	53.35
3. A. C. Nesty (SUR)	53.41
4. P. Khnykine (EUN)	53.81
5. M. Stewart (USA)	54.04
6. M. Gery (CAN)	54.18

4 x 100m medley

Men	31.07.1992
1. USA	WR 3:36.93
Rouse · Diebel Morales · Olsen	
2. EUN	3:38.56
Selkov · Ivanov Khnykine · Popov	
3. CAN	3:39.66
Tewksbury · Cleveland Gery · Clark	
4. GER	3:40.19
5. FRA	3:40.51
6. HUN	3:42.03

200m butterfly

Men	30.07.1992
1. M. Stewart (USA)	1:56.26
2. D. J. Loader (NZL)	1:57.93
3. F. Esposito (FRA)	1:58.51
4. R. Szukala (POL)	1:58.89
5. K. Kawanaka (JPN)	1:58.97
6. D. Pankratov (EUN)	1:58.98

The gymnast from another planet

Judges decisions are often criticised by those who think they know better, but it seems that in the men's gymnastics event, their scoring was particularly difficult to understand. Despite the brilliant displays by 20-year-old Vitaly Scherbo, which bordered on perfection, it seemed that nothing he did, would get him awarded the perfect ten. He moved with an elegance and poise that even outclassed the assembled world élite. He won six out of a possible eight gold medals, yet was steadfastly denied the dream mark of ten. Never before had a gymnast so dominated his sport as did Vitaly Scherbo at the Olympic Games. The son of an artist from Kherson in Byelorussia, Scherbo was the last rising star of the Russian school which, under the leadership of its chief trainer, Leonid Arkayev, has dominated men's gymnastics for decades. Of course, there were other victors in the men's gymnastics event. They hailed from Japan and China, from the former GDR as well as from Hungary, Italy and the USA, but they were isolated cases. The dominance of the former USSR was demonstrated clearly in the team all-round competition.

Unified Team still dominates

Since its first victory in 1952, the Soviet team has not lost a single final in 40 years. Only once did it fail to appear on the winner's rostrum, and that was in 1984 when the USSR boycotted the games in Los Angeles. In Barcelona too, the Unified Team was way ahead of the rest of the world. It beat the silver medallist from China by more than five points, due in no small measure to Vitaly Scherbo's outstanding performance. This was the last appearance of the team once celebrated as the Soviets, which was competing for the first and last time under the name of the Unified Team. In future, the athletes will be competing for their own countries – Byelorussia in Vitaly Scherbo's case. Scherbo was not yet sure in his hour of triumph whether he would actually continue to live there. After all, he had received some tempting offers. The USA and

Despite some amazing somersaults on the vault, the Japanese Yutaka Aihara did not make it on to the podium.

A gymnast for the connoisseur: Vitaly Scherbo deserved all the superlatives.

Two schools of gymnastics and two different styles. Xioasahuang Li from China on the pommel horse (below) and Vitaly Scherbo on the rings (above).

Japan were enticing him with highly-paid contracts, while his personal choice tended towards Sweden. Since the political changes, no doors are barred to Scherbo, unlike former Olympic teams from the former Eastern bloc. Scherbo has a dashing, confident manner and has long cultivated a cosmopolitan lifestyle.

Dazzling comeback for Wecker

Scherbo seemed to be prepared for the change in circumstances, in contrast to the German Andreas Wecker. Following the upheavals, this champion gymnast from the former GDR had at first shown a dete-

rioration in form, but in Barcelona he managed a dazzling comeback. The 22-year-old had prepared conscientiously, and was the only gymnast in the world to perform a double Kovac somersault on the high bar. Gold appeared within his grasp, but a small sidestep on landing, as he tried to make a triple somersault, handed victory to the American Trent Dimas. However, he won a silver on the bar, bronze on the pommel horse and on the rings, as well as fourth place in the all-round category behind three gymnasts from the Unified Team. His successes made plain that he had overcome his crisis.

Germany's Andreas Wecker
(below and bottom left) and
Igor Korobtchinski (right) gave a
demonstration of precision and
daring.

No child's play for Tatyana

Had Svetlana Boginskaya not been there, it would probably not have occurred to anyone that the term women's gymnastics as witnessed on the equipment of the Palau Sant Jordi only bore any resemblance to traditional concepts of gymnastics, when the Germans were perform-

ing. They recalled only too clearly the level prevalent at country fairs and consequently occupied the lowest places in the results tables. The élite from the Unified Team, comprising the CIS and Georgia, Hungary, Romania, the USA and China, on the other hand, demonstrated more clearly than ever

before how far this Olympic event has changed in recent years. It has been elevated to an audacious, breathtaking spectacle of artistry and acrobatics, an expression of grace and elegance. Feats of the greatest difficulty followed one another at a breathless pace, performed with precision and imagination by young girls about to flower into womanhood. Many of the competitors were 16 years old or even younger. Some were barely 1.40 metres tall and weighed hardly more than 35 kilos. The tension of the event showed in their faces, though in the past these young ath-

The girls are usually no more than 15 years old. They weigh around six stone and are about 4ft 6ins tall They perform their exercises, as if nothing else mattered apart from their vault, beam and gymnastics mat, or their parallel and asymmetrical bars. The serious way, in which they approach their sport, is no different to the way little girls play with their doll's house. The chances are though that these girls never played with a doll's house, because, for the past eight or nine years, they have scarcely had any time to do anything else apart from gymnastics. They have almost become dolls themselves. Their hair is beautifully trimmed and they wear grown-ups' make-up. They are the prettiest pixies in the world and yet, at some time in the last few years, they have probably injured either their leg, their knee, their back, their shoulders or their hand. They all say how much they enjoy the swinging, the twisting and the other complex movements. They all say how much they delight in showing off their graceful skills, which combine elements of dance, drama, music and gymnastics. And, of course, it makes sense. After all, tumbling on the mat and performing acrobatic somersaults is much more fun than sitting in a maths lesson. They have done it by devoting an enormous amount of time and energy. The new queen of the gymnasts, who showed off her graceful skills to Barcelona's San Jordi Palace, is called Tatyana Gutsu. She comes from the Ukraine and is 15 years old.

And they call that fun? Tatyana Lyssenko, Bo Yang and Kim Zmeskal (left to right) display their talents on the beam..

letes showed incredible sang-froid. For instance, in Los Angeles in 1984, just as Ecaterina Szabo of Romania was about to step into the arena, a power failure darkened the hall. Despite the fact that she needed a perfect ten to win the event, Szabo kept her cool and achieved this incredible score.

The return of veteran Svetlana Boginskaya

This year, Svetlana Boginskaya of the Unified Team, competed as a veteran. She had been the darling of the Seoul public in 1988, winning two gold medals (on the vault and in the team event), a silver and a bronze. She was three times World and eight times European champion. In Barcelona too, she won the sympathy of the public. At

1.61 metres tall and weighing 47 kilograms, she was the heaviest and the tallest woman gymnast and yet the only one who could combine acrobatics with dance movement, using grace and skill. The judges were not so impressed. Boginskaya only won in the team event, taking no medals in the individual competitions. She came fourth on the vault and fifth, both on the beam and in the all-round category.

Just a bronze for Kim Zmeskal

Her great rival of previous years, the American, Kim Zmeskal, fared even worse. Although this power house from Houston, Texas embodied, like no other the new type of woman gymnast, her only medal was a bronze in the team event.

Victory at Barcelona went to the other Unified Team favourite, Tatyana Gutsu, a flaxen-haired teenager from Odessa in the Ukraine. A fall from the beam in the team final had blown her chances of participating in the individual all-round competition. Then her team-mate, Rozalie Galieva, was declared injured at short notice and Tatyana Gutsu was allowed to take her place. She was rewarded two days later with victory in the team competition. Counted among the other medal-winners were the Romanian, Lavinia Milosovici, the Hungarian, Henrietta Onodi, Li Lu from China and Shannon Miller from the USA. Whether any of them will be able to emulate the outstanding performance of Svetlana Boginskaya in future years remains to be seen.

Kim Zmeskal (above), one of the American team gymnasts on the beam. In the end, the Unified Team's overall talent prevailed.

First hold on tightly and then comes the reward: gold for Tatiana Lyssenko (left).

One reigned supreme over all
others: Alexandra Timochenko
(below), who crowned an
unparalleled career with her
Olympic victory.

Awed silence for Alexandra

Normally, the Spanish spectators are only interested in contestants from their own country. The more so, when Spanish athletes are still in with a chance of a medal. But when the 20 year-old Alexandra Timochenko (CIS) stepped out on to the mat, even the Spanish were hushed into awed silence. There have been many good gymnasts in the short history of rhythmic gymnastics. But none have made anything like the sort of impact on this sport as the young lady from Kiev. Ever since she won the bronze medal in Seoul, she has developed an unstoppable momentum towards being the world's number one. Her victory at the Barcelona Olympics was really no more than official confirmation of her exceptional status. For as Alexandra Timochenko stepped out on to the mat, the 6,500 spectators stepped with her into a completely different world. A world of grace and elegance, entranced by the magically flowing lightness and harmony of all her movements. Timochenko seemed to be just like a ballerina as she went gliding through her routine, which was packed with movements of the utmost difficulty. But whereas her competitor's routines often seemed no more than the concatenation of isolated elements, Alexandra Timochenko made the spectators forget completely that she was engaged in any sort of competitive gymnastics at all, that her perfect grace was the result of immensely hard work. In the words of her coach, Irina Derjugina, "Alexandra is unique and will remain so."

Only Oksana Skaldina (centre left) was able to keep up with her friend Alexandra Timochenko. For years, the two of them have dominated rhythmic gymnastics.

Elegance and grace using difficult apparatus: the Bulgarian Maria Petrova (far left and below) and Joana Bodak from Poland (above).

RESULTS

Whether as the former USSR or now as the CIS - they were simply unbeatable: Valeri Belenki, Grigori Misioutine and Vitaly Scherbo (left to right).

A giant among dwarves: Bela Karolyi, the world's most successful trainer of gymnasts, giving last words of advice to Kerri Strong.

Li Lu from China embodies the gymnast of the future: immense strength contained in a remarkably compact body.

The outsider who scored gold: Trent Dimas (USA) was victorious on the horizontal bars.

Horizontal bar

Men	02.08.1992
1. T. Dimas (USA)	9.875
2. G. Misioutine (EUN)	9.837
2. A. Wecker (GER)	9.837
4. L. Guo (CHN)	9.812
5. V. Belenki (EUN)	9.787
5. Y. Hatakeda (JPN)	9.787

All-round

Men	31.07.1992
1. V. Scherbo (EUN)	59.025
2. G. Misioutine (EUN)	58.925
3. V. Belenki (EUN)	58.625
4. A. Wecker (GER)	58.450
5. X. Li (CHN)	58.150
6. L. Guo (CHN)	57.925

Team

Men	29.07.1992
1. EUN	585.450
Scherbo · Belenki · Korobtchinski Misioutin · Shapirov · Woropaiev	
2. CHN	580.375
X. Li · D. Li · Guo · C. Li J. Li · G. Li	
3. JAP	578.250
Nishikawa · Iketani · Hatakeda Chinen · Aihara · Matsunaga	
4. GER	575.575
5. ITA	571.750
6. USA	571.725

Floor

Men	04.08.1992
1. X. Li (CHN)	9.925
2. Y. Iketani (JPN)	9.787
2. G. Misioutine (EUN)	9.787
4. Ok Ryul Yoo (KOR)	9.775
5. Y. Aihara (JPN)	9.737
6. V. Chtcherbo (EUN)	9.712
7. A. Wecker (GER)	9.687
8. C. Li (CHN)	9.387

Rings

Men	02.08.1992
1. V. Scherbo (EUN)	9.937
2. J. Li (CHN)	9.875
3. X. Li (CHN)	9.862
3. A. Wecker (GER)	9.862
5. V. Belenki (EUN)	9.825
6. S. Csollany (HUN)	9.800
7. Y. Iketani (JPN)	9.762
8. K. P. Khristozov (BUL)	9.750

Parallel bars

Men	02.08.1992
1. V. Scherbo (EUN)	9.900
2. J. Li (CHN)	9.812
3. L. Guo (CHN)	9.800
3. I. Korobtchinski (EUN)	9.800
3. M. Matsunaga (JPN)	9.800
6. J. Lynch (USA)	9.712

Pommel horse

Men	02.08.1992
1. V. Scherbo (EUN)	9.925
1. Gil-Su Faz (PRK)	9.925
3. A. Wecker (GER)	9.875
4. L. Guo (CHN)	9.800
5. M. C. Waller (USA)	9.825
6. Y. Hatakeda (JPN)	9.775

Vault

Men	02.08.1992
1. V. Scherbo (EUN)	9.856
2. G. Misioutine (EUN)	9.781
3. Ok Ryul Yoo (KOR)	9.762
4. X. Li (CHN)	9.731
5. Z. Supola (HUN)	9.674
6. S. Kroll (GER)	9.662
7. S. Csollany (HUN)	9.524
8. Y. Aihara (JPN)	9.450

The best performers in the all round: Lavinia Milosovici, Tatiana Goutsou and Shannon Miller.

Andreas Wecker was the one German athelete who managed to break through the massed ranks of victorious Russians and Asians.

Shannon Miller's successes were enough to enthuse even the otherwise self-controlled American coach, Bela Karolyi.

Grace, elegance, muscle-power and forceful sommersaults: the performance on the floor by Lavinia Milosovici was a perfect one that deserved perfect marks.

All-round

Women	30.07.1992
1. T. Goutsou (EUN)	39.735
2. S. Miller (USA)	39.725
3. L. Milosovici (ROM)	39.687
4. C. Bontas (ROM)	39.674
5. S. Boguinskaia (EUN)	39.673
6. G. Gogean (ROM)	39.624
7. T. Lyssenko (EUN)	39.537
8. H. Onodi (HUN)	39.449
9. S. Fraguas (ESP)	39.424

Floor

Women	01.08.1992
1. L. C. Milosovici (ROM)	10.000
2. H. Onodi (HUN)	9.950
3. T. Goutsou (ROM)	9.912
3. C. Bontas (ROM)	9.912
3. S. Miller (USA)	9.912
6. K. Zmeskal (USA)	9.900

Team

Women	29.07.1992
1. EUN	395.666
Boginskaja · Galijeva · Gutsu Grudneva · Lyssenko · Tshussovitina	
2. ROM	395.079
Bontas · Gogeean · Hadarean Milososvici · Neculita · Pasca	
3. USA	394.704
Bruce · Dawes · Miller · Okino Strug · Smeskal	
4. CHN	392.941
5. ESP	391.428
8. FRA	386.052

Asymmetric bars

Women	01.08.1992
1. L. Lu (CHN)	10.000
2. T. Goutsou (EUN)	9.975
3. S. Miller (USA)	9.962
4. Gwang-Suk Kim (PRK)	9.912
4. L. C. Milosovici (ROM)	9.912
4. M. A. Pasca (ROM)	9.912

Beam

Women	01.08.1992
1. T. Lyssenko (EUN)	9.975
2. L. Lu (CHN)	9.912
2. S. Miller (USA)	9.912
4. C. Bontas (ROM)	9.875
5. S. Boguinskaia (EUN)	9.862
6. B. Okino (USA)	9.837
7. B. Yang (CHN)	9.300
8. L. C. Milosovici (ROM)	9.262

Rhythmic all-round

Women	08.08.1992
1. A. Timoshenko (EUN)	59.037
2. C. Pascual (ESP)	58.100
3. O. Skaldina (EUN)	57.912
4. C. Acedo (ESP)	57.225
5. M. Petrova (BUL)	57.087
6. I. Deleanu (ROM)	56.612
7. J. Bodak (POL)	56.475
8. L. Oulehlova (TCH)	56.137

Vault

Women	01.08.1992
1. H. Onodi (HUN)	9.925
1. L. C. Milosovici (ROM)	9.925
3. T. Lyssenko (EUN)	9.912
4. S. Boguinskaia (EUN)	9.899
5. G. Gogean (ROM)	9.893
6. S. Miller (USA)	9.837

British men row the golds home

Cox, Terence Michael Paul, gets a soaking. The Canadian eights rowed their boat home for the gold medal.

Reprise. Thomas Lange repeated his success at Seoul. He came home well ahead of the competition in the single sculls.

As with so many amateur sports, it was the British who turned rowing into a competitive sport. The University boat race, the Henley regatta are national institutions. It is only to be expected that Britain has been one of the most successful nations with a creditable medals total accumulated over the 92 years since the event was first introduced. In recent years, however, the eastern European nations have devoted a lot of resources to the sport and the German team, with many of the former East Germans in their side were destined to take a high proportion of the 8 men's medals and 6 women's medals on offer.

The venue for the Barcelona Games was a lake at Banyoles, 70 km north of the city. The races cover a distance of over 2,000 metres and the six finalists have to compe-

te in heats, semi-finals and what is known as the repêchage. The repêchage races are for those crews who do not qualify directly for the next round. They provide a safeguard to ensure that crews with medal potential do not get eliminated too early, because they were drawn into an unfairly tough opening heat.

There are two distinct rowing categories. There is sweep rowing, where the oarsman uses a single oar two-handed, as in coxless and coxed pairs, coxless and coxed fours and eights and sculling, where two oars are used by each crew member, as in single, double or quadruple sculling.

The outstanding name in British rowing is Steve Redgrave. He has an international success record which takes some beating. Before Barcelona, he already had three Olympic medals - two golds from the 1984 coxed four and the 1988 coxless pairs together with the bronze in the Seoul coxless pairs Added to which are a host of medals in the Commonwealth Games and the world championships. After the 1988 Olympics, he split up with Andy Holmes and started a new partnership with Matthew Pinsent, but the success story continued. Victory in Barcelona in the coxless pairs gave Redgrave his third consecutive Olympic gold medal, a feat never achieved by a British oarsman. One Jack Beres-

Britain's Steven Redgrave and Matthew Pinsent could hardly believe it. The British oarsmen made it two in a row in the coxless pairs.

Top right: The Searle brothers embrace their cox, Garry Herbert. The threesome won Britain's second rowing gold in the coxed pairs.

ford took three gold medals between the wars, but not consecutively.

Effortless progress

Having reached the finals more or less effortlessly, Redgrave and Pinsent crossed the finishing line seven seconds inside the old record and five seconds clear of all opposition. While Pinsent could not restrain his emotions, Redgrave simply leaned forward and patted his partner on the shoulder. It was a controlled reaction and out of keeping with the excitement of the Olympic circus. Once again, his meticulous preparation had not let him down. It was difficult to see what could prevent Redgrave from achieving a fourth gold four years hence. And yet, only 10 weeks prior to the Games, Redgrave had been wea-

kened by a bowel inflammation and the pair were losing races. Their training programme, which was masterminded by the German, Jurgen Gröbler, was a horrifying test of endurance and the results that should have flowed from that, did not materialise. Ironically, the disruption to their work gave them a psychological boost as they were no longer regarded as favourites. But the testing régime soon started to yield results. Gröbler maintained that they were half a per cent faster than last year.

In the Vienna world championship, they had set the fastest ever time, but in Barcelona, they were six seconds outside that time. But it was clear that the British pair were in complete control. They crossed the finishing line, a line of bubbles in the water, with confidence and

had scarcely looked threatened. Initially, the German pair had taken a small lead and they and the Slovenes tried to hang on to the British pair, but after a minute, Redgrave and Pinsent showed in front. The effort was maintained for three quarters of the race, with Redgrave calling for more push to get clear, but it was so obvious that they had not given their all. Gröbler claimed that his men could have taken another three seconds off the Olympic record.

Searle brothers celebrate a golden weekend

The day after Redgrave and Pinsent had overwhelmed their opponents in the coxless pairs, the Searle brothers wrote another story for the Boys' Own paper. The two young men, Greg, 20 and Jonny, 23,

Three men and a boat

from Chertsey, gave Britain its second rowing gold in a spectacular fashion. They overcame two Italian brothers, Carmine and Giuseppe Abbagnale, who had an impressive record, having been gold medallists twice and world champions seven times. Coming from behind in the coxed pairs, the two brothers won the race in the last few strokes of the race. The Italians had built up a four second advantage at the half-way stage and looked to be holding off a challenge from the Romanian pair. The two Surrey students were regarded as novices and yet, they exuded a confidence, which shocked the experienced Italians, equally confidently looking to their hat-trick of Olympic titles. Their drive to the finishing line, which cut the deficit of a boat's length in the last 200 metres, was one of the most exciting moments in the rowing events and certainly a contrast to Redgrave and Pinsent's comfortable victory in the coxless pairs

The intensity of the struggle in the last few metres was such that a man from both the Italian and Romanian boats, the silver and bronze medal winners, had to be hauled out of their boats by crews on the ambulance launch. Underlining the brothers' effort, their cox, Garry Herbert, a history student, said: "I wanted them to be prepared to die for us, and they nearly did".

The North Americans dominated the coxless fours. The Canadian crew beat the Americans, with the Germans taking the bronze.

Three men were enjoying the sun at Banyoles lake, a three-hour drive from Barcelona. One of them was Peter Michael Kolbe. He had considerable success as a rower, but retired a few years ago. He is now the director of the German Rowing Association. The second man was his rival, the Finn, Pertti Karppinen. That morning, he had come fourth in the B final. Karppinen is 39 years old. The third man was Thomas Lange, aged 28, from Halle an der Saale, in what used to be known as East Germany. He had crossed the finishing line a full length ahead of his nearest rival. Three times world champion and gold medallist in Seoul, Herr Lange is used to success, but this time it was different. Things have changed so much for this young man in the last two or three years. Political changes have caused a few domestic problems, even in the most tightly-knit families, That was certainly the case for Thomas Lange. A career in rowing does not bring home the bacon, so he resumed his medical training. But then one day, he decided to take a term off from his studies, he returned to his boat, and found himself a sponsor. Thomas Lange could have regaled bystanders with an account of the past few months in his life, as he received his gold medal. He has had to adapt himself to the values of another society, almost another world and he has come to accept them.

Three rowers, three worlds. One of the enduring qualities of sport is its ability to compress a whole life into a small space of time.

Kerstin Köppen and Kathrin Boron of the German team look exhausted after winning the gold medal in the double sculls.

Man overboard. One of the Canadian winning eights team carries the flag.

French coxless pairs duo, Christine Gosse and Isabelle Danjou look dejected after just missing out on a medal. They came fourth.

Double sculls

Men	01.08.1992
1. AUS Hawkins · Antonie	6:17.32
2. AUT Jonke · Zerbst	6:18.42
3. NED Zwolle · Rienks	6:22.82
4. EST Tasane · Lutoskin	6:23.34
5. NOR Marszalek · Krzepinski	6:24.32

Coxless pairs

Men	01.08.1992
1. GBR Redgrave · Pinsent	6:27.72
2. GER Hoeltzenbein · von Ettingshausen	6:32.68
3. SLO Cop · Zvegelj	6:33.43
4. FRA Andrieux · Rolland	6:36.34
5. BEL van Driessche · Goiris	6:38.20

Single sculls

Men	01.08.1992
1. T. Lange (GER)	6:51.40
2. V. Chalupa (TCH)	6:52.93
3. K. Broniewski (POL)	6:56.82
4. E. F. Verdonk (NZL)	6:57.45
5. J. Jaanson (EST)	7:12.92
6. S. Fernandez (ARG)	7:15.53

Coxed pairs

Men	02.08.1992
1. GBR Searle · Searle Herbert	6:49.83
2. ITA Abbagnale · Abbagnale di Capua	6:50.98
3. ROM Popescu · Taga Raducanu	6:51.58
4. GER	6:56.98
5. CUB	6:58.26
6. FRA	7:03.01

Coxless fours

Men	02.08.1992
1. AUS Cooper · McKay Green · Tomkins	5:55.04
2. USA Burden · McLaughlin Bohrer · Manning	5:56.68
3. SLO Klemencic · Mirjanic Jansa · Mujkic	5:58.24
4. GER	5:58.39
5. NED	5:59.14
6. NZL	6:02.13

Coxed fours

Men	01.08.1992
1. ROM Talapan · Ruican · Popescu Taga · Raducanu	5:59.37
2. GER Kellner · Brudel · Peters Finger · Reiher	6:00.34
3. POL Streich · Jankowski · Tomiak Lasicki · Cieslak	6:03.27
4. USA	6:06.03
5. FRA	6:06.82
6. EUN	6:12.13

Eights

Men	02.08.1992
1. CAN	5:29.53
2. ROM	5:29.67
3. GER	5:31.00
4. USA	5:33.18
5. AUS	5:33.72
6. GBR	5:39.92

Quadruple sculls

Men	02.08.1992
1. GER Willms · Hajek Volkert · Steinbach	5:45.17
2. NOR Bjonness · Thorsen Undset · Saetersdal	5:47.09
3. ITA Farina · Galtarossa Corona · Soffici	5:47.33
4. SUI	5:47.39
5. NED	5:48.92
6. FRA	5:54.80

The Australian men's coxless fours team (above) after the successful row for gold. Exhausted but delighted, the Romanian Elisabeta Lipa after her triumph in the single sculls.

Stefanie Werremeier and Ingeborg Schwermann congratulate each other after coming in second in the women's coxless pairs (above).

They had their ups and downs, but the German quadruple sculls team eventually created an effective unit... and won the gold.

Coxless pairs

Women	01.08.1992
1. CAN McBean · Heddle	7:06.22
2. GER Werremeier · Schwerzmann	7:07.96
3. USA Seaton · Pierson	7:08.11
4. FRA Gosse · Danjou	7:08.70
5. GBR Turvey · Batten	7:17.28

Double sculls

Women	01.08.1992
1. GER Köppen · Boron	6:49.00
2. ROM Cochelea · Lipa	6:51.47
3. CHN Gu · Lu	6:55.16
4. NZL Baker · Lawson	6:56.81
5. GBR Eyres · Gill	7:06.62

Coxless fours

Women	01.08.1992
1. CAN Barnes · Taylor Monroe · Worthington	6:30.85
2. USA Donohoe · Eckert Fuller · Feeney	6:31.86
3. GER Frank · Mehl Siech · Hohn	6:32.34
4. CHN	6:32.50
5. ROM	6:37.24
6. AUS	6:41.72

Quadruple sculls

Women	02.08.1992
1. GER Müller · Schmidt Peter · Mundt	6:20.18
2. ROM Pipota · Ignat Cochelea · Dobre	6:24.34
3. EUN Khodotovitch · Zelikovitch Oustioujanina · Khloptseva	6:25.07
4. NED	6:32.40
5. USA	6:32.65
6. TCH	6:35.99

Single sculls

Women	02.08.1992
1. E. Lipa (ROM)	7:25.54
2. A. Bredael (BEL)	7:26.64
3. S. S. Laumann (CAN)	7:28.85
4. A. Marden (USA)	7:29.84
5. M. Brandin (SWE)	7:37.55
6. C. le Moal (FRA)	7:41.85

Eights

Women	02.08.1992
1. CAN	6:02.62
2. ROM	6:06.26
3. GER	6:07.80
4. EUN	6:09.68
5. CHN	6:12.08
6. USA	6:12.25

The German canoe-
ists left all others
behind: gold for their
kayak fours (left)
and for the paddling
housewife Birgit
Schmidt (right).

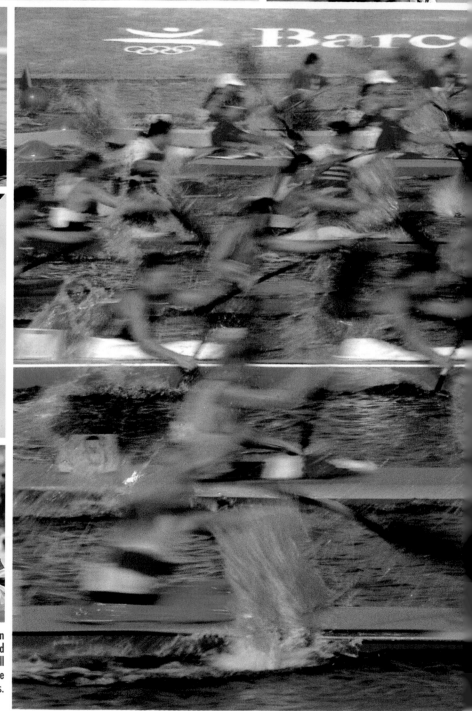

Hoyer and Boivin
(FRA, above, inset)
paddled into sixth
place, Ramona
Portwich and Anke
von Seck (above)
scored gold.

Twice Olympic victory made in
Potsdam: Kay Bluhm and
Torsten Gutsche left behind all
kayak competition both over the
500 and 1000 metres.

A silver lining for Mariott

Only a whisker lay between Britain's Gareth Mariott and the gold medal in the C1 canoe slalom. Most people watching did not see the fateful pole move. Doubtless it did, but Marriott seemed equally unware of it, racing on indomitably to win the silver. His approach during the pre-Olympic competition, to go for speed rather than spend precious time testing out the course, so nearly paid off. It certainly led him to win the pre-Olympic competition as well as the current World Championship.

The competition proved a bigger disappointment for Britain's other great hopeful, Richard Fox,. Fox has always raced in the more universally popular kayak (K1) and narrowly missed a medal by being placed fourth in this event. The performance of the remainder of the British K1 team, Melvyn Jones and Ian Raspin, who were ranked seventh and twentieth respectively in Barcelona, must raise serious questions about the judgement of the selectors in choosing to leave at home the current world K1 slalom champion, Shaun Pearce, whatever the scores in the selection event. This was the first Olympics since Munich in 1972 to include slalom events, although flat water sprint canoeing - not a British strength - has been on the programme since 1936. The costs involved in constructing the artificial slalom course, in which the water flow can be controlled so that all competitors face identical conditions, is too high for nations not likely to make substantial use of it afterwards.

Canoeists on their way in search of medals (left). Spelley and Papke (above left) managed to score twice: silver in the 500 m and gold in the 1000 m.

RESULTS

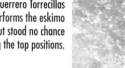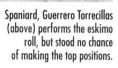

Spaniard, Guerrero Torrecillas (above) performs the eskimo roll, but stood no chance of making the top positions.

French canoeist, Sylvain Curinier (above) at the Seu d"Urgell. She took the silver medal in the women's slalom.

Adison and Forgues, the two French bronze medallists in the slalom kayak doubles.

K 1	500 m
Men	*07.08.1992*
1. M. Y. Kolehmainen (FIN)	1:40.34
2. Z. Gyulay (HUN)	1:40.64
3. K. Holman (NOR)	1:40.71
4. N. Bellingham (USA)	1:40.84
5. S. Kalesnik (EUN)	1:40.90
6. R. Liberato (SUI)	1:41.98

K 2	1000 m
Men	*08.08.1992*
1. C. Robinson (AUS)	3:37.26
2. K. Holmann (NOR)	3:37.50
3. G. Barton (USA)	3:37.93
4. M. G. Popescu (ROM)	3:38.37
5. B. Bonomi (ITA)	3:41.12
6. J. Garcia (POR)	3:41.60
7. T. Nielsen (DEN)	3:41.70
8. R. J. Crichlow (CAN)	3:43.46
9. A. Vieta (LIT)	3:46.92

K 2	1000 m
Men	*08.08.1992*
1. GER Bluhm · Gutsche	3:16.10
2. SWE Olsson · Sundqvist	3:17.70
3. POL Kotowicz · Bialkowski	3:18.86

K 2	500 m
Men	*07.08.1992*
1. GER Bluhm · Gutsche	1:28.27
2. POL Freimut · Kurpiewski	1:29.84
3. ITA Rossi · Dreossi	1:30.00
4. ESP	1:30.93
5. SWE	1:31.48
6. DEN	1:31.84

K 4	1000 m
Men	*08.08.1992*
1. GER von Appen · Kegel Reineck · Wohllebe	2:54.18
2. HUN Csipes · Gyulay Fidel · Abraham	2:54.82
3. AUS Graham · Rowling Wood · Andersson	2:56.97
4. TCH	2:57.06
5. ROM	3:00.11
6. POL	3:01.43

C 1	500 m
Men	*07.08.1992*
1. N. Boukhalov (BUL)	1:51.15
2. M. Sliwinski (EUN)	1:51.40
3. O. Heukrodt (GER)	1:53.00
4. S. Knazovicky (TCH)	1:54.51
5. I. Pulai (HUN)	1:54.86
6. S. C. Giles (CAN)	1:55.80

C 1	1000 m
Men	*08.08.1992*
1. N. Boukhalov (BUL)	4:05.92
2. I. Klementjevs (LAT)	4:06.60
3. G. Zala (HUN)	4:07.35
4. M. Röder (GER)	4:08.96
5. P. Sylvoz (FRA)	4:09.82
6. A. J. Train (GBR)	4:12.58
7. V. Partnoi (ROM)	4:14.27
8. J. Bartunek (TCH)	4:15.25
9. S. C. Giles (CAN)	4:17.12

C 2	500 m
Men	*07.08.1992*
1. EUN Masseikov · Dovgalenok	1:41.54
2. GER Papke · Spelly	1:41.68
3. BUL Marinov · Stoyanov	1:41.94

C 2	1000 m
Men	*08.08.1992*
1. GER Papke · Spelly	3:37.42
2. DEN Nielsson · Frederiksen	3:39.26
3. FRA Hoyer · Boivin	3:39.51

Briton, Gareth Marriott in a tricky manoeuvre on the white-water.

Fast-flowing waters. The American men Scott Strausbaugh and Joe Jacobi on the gold trail.

...nchman Avril had difficulty ...ing with the technically ...manding slalom course.

K 1		500 m
Women		07.08.1992
1. B. Schmidt (GER)		1:51.60
2. R. Koban (HUN)		1:51.96
3. I. Dylewska (POL)		1:52.36
4. J. Idem (ITA)		1:52.78
5. U. Profanter (AUT)		1:53.17
6. S. Goetschy (FRA)		1:53.53
7. C. Brunet (CAN)		1:54.82
8. S. Toma (ROM)		1:54.84
9. S. Gunnarsson (SWE)		1:55.55

K 1		Slalom
Women		01.08.1992
1. E. Micheler (GER)		126.41
2. D. Woodward (AUS)		128.27
3. D. Chladek (USA)		131.75
4. E. Roth (GER)		132.29
5. M. Agulhon (FRA)		132.89
6. K. Striepecke (GER)		134.49

K 1		Slalom
Men		02.08.1992
1. P. Ferrazzi (ITA)		106.89
2. S. Curinier (FRA)		107.06
3. J. Lettmann (GER)		108.52
4. R. Fox (GBR)		108.85
5. L. Brissaud (FRA)		109.37
6. M. Strukelj (SLO)		110.11

C 2		Slalom
Men		02.08.1992
1. USA Strausbaugh · Jacobi		122.41
2. TCH Simek · Rohan		124.25
3. FRA Adisson · Forgues		124.38
4. USA McEwan · Haller		128.05
5. SUI Matti · Matti		128.55

C 1		Slalom
Men		01.08.1992
1. L. Pollert (TCH)		113.69
2. G. Marriott (GBR)		116.48
3. J. Avril (FRA)		117.18
4. J. Lugbill (USA)		118.62
5. R. de Monti (ITA)		119.02
6. M. Lang (GER)		119.19

K 4		500 m
Women		08.08.1992
1. HUN Donusz · Czingay Meszaros · Koban		1:38.32
2. GER Portwich · von Seck Schmidt · Borchert		1:38.47
3. SWE Olsson · Haglund Rosenqvist · Andersson		1:39.79
4. ROM		1:41.02
5. CHN		1:41.12
6. CAN		1:42.28

K 2		500 m
Women		07.08.1992
1. GER Portwich · von Seck		1:40.29
2. SWE Gunnarsson · Andersson		1:40.41
3. HUN Koban · Donusz		1:40.81
4. ROM		1:42.12
5. CAN		1:42.14
6. POL		1:42.44
7. CHN		1:42.46
8. DEN		1:43.98

Lawrie's crew bring in the bronze

In the Soling class, Britain's crew captained by Lawrie Smith won Britain's only medal in the yachting, a bronze.

In the Flying Dutchman, the four-times German world championship team could only manage a disappointing fifth position.

The morning after winning Britain's sole Olympic sailing medal, Lawrie Smith put his very satisfying performance in perspective:

"We only spent six months and we won a bronze medal. That's good value, isn't it?"

There are 10 yachting events and Britain had entered a team with hopes of winning four or five medals, but apart from skipper Smith and his crew of Rob Cruikshank and Ossie Stewart, the final outcome was disappointing. The British coach, Rod Carr, was ready to give his opinion on the disappointing outcome. The reason, he said, had much to do with the British climate. In short, the Mediterranean is not the English Channel. But what puts the British team at a severe disadvantage is the absence of any leagues, local, regional or national. That would provide the competitive edge that is missing from the British sailing scene.

Nevertheless, a British medal in the Soling class was an historic achievement. Soling is the largest of the Olympic classes with three-man boats designed for sea-going racing. Britain came fourth in this class in 1988, so Smith's bronze was a logical step forward. In the competition itself, Smith's crew won their first race for the bronze, was outclassed in the second and won the decider by less than a boat-

Round the buoy. In the windsurfing class, Frenchman Franck David took the gold coming ahead of an American and an Australian.

length. In the 470 event, Paul Brotherton and Andy Hemmings let the pressure upset their composure and took too many risks. Stuart Childerley went for gold or broke in the Finn and got broke. Penny Way, a good prospect in the Lechner or windsurfing as current world champion, seemed to lack confidence and her male counterpart Barrie Edgington was disappointing.

In many Olympic Games, the sailing events are relegated to some off-shore spot, miles from the main arenas. In Seoul, the event was held 250 miles from the capital and in Atlanta in 1996, the boat crews will again be hundreds of miles away in steamy-hot Savannah. This year, however, the sailing was centre-stage, in the Port Olimpic right next to the Olympic Village.

The public were offered a grandstand view, with a pier built out specially into the water, though for security reasons in the end it was only available to those with accred-

itation. One event, the Soling class, was held close inshore, so that the public had a good view. This was one of the few events in which Spain did not do well. It was won by the Dane, Jesper Bank, with Kevin Mahaney of the USA winning the silver, and Britain, of course, gaining its lone bronze medal. The Germans suffered a series of mishaps in these events in which the rules are so complex , it is hard even for the competitors to understand them. In the women's 470 Class, Christina Pinnow's life-jacket was found to be 30 grammes overweight and in the 470 class, Wolfgang Hunger and Rolf Schmidt were disqualified for an early start and then suffered a torn spinaker. "After that we could only do better," explained Hunger, who came third in two other races, but finished eighth in the overall standings.

The men's windsurfing proved to be the most exciting event. Although Franck David of France was in the

lead in the finals, Mike Gebhardt of the USA, who was coming up fast behind him, had been the overnight winner. In the end, Gebhardt only won a bronze.

The women's windsurfing event, held for the first time, proved to be a family affair. Barbara Kendall of New Zealand, who won the gold, is the sister of Bruce Kendall, gold medal-winner in Seoul in the men's windsurfing.

The Star class was won by the American Mark Reynolds, who beat his former fellow-countryman, Rod Davis. Davis had won a gold in the Soling in 1984 as an American, but has since emigrated and is now a New Zealander.

The dominance of the hosts

The Spaniards had every reason to be proud of their crews, and not only because a member of the Spanish royal family, Crown Prince Felipe, was skippering a Spanish craft. However, the first Spanish gold was not won by the standard-

Albert Batzill and Peter Lang, four-time world champions in the Flying Dutchman class, started out as favourites, but disappointingly ended up fifth.

The two man Star boats in the waters off Parc de Mar.

Windsurfing

Women　　　　02.08.1992

1. B. A. Kendall (NZL)
2. X. Zhang (CHN)
3. D. de Vries (NED)
4. M. Herbert (FRA)
5. L. Butler (USA)
6. P. Way (GBR)

470

Women　　　　03.08.1992

1. Zabell · Guerra (ESP)
2. Egnot · Shearer (NZL)
3. Isler · Healey (USA)
4. Moscalenko · Pakholtchik (EUN)
5. Shige · Kinoshita (JPN)
6. Le Brun · Barre (FRA)
7. Quarra · Barabino (ITA)
8. Hardwiger · Pinnow (GER)
9. Lidgett · Bucek (AUS)
10. Laike · Slunga-Tallberg (FIN)

Europe

Women　　　　03.08.1992

1. L. Andersen (NOR)
2. N. v. Dufresne (ESP)
3. J. Trotman (USA)
4. J. Armstrong (NZL)
5. D. Jensen (DEN)
6. K. Kruuv (EST)

British judo quartet on the podium

Many people would be surprised to know that Britain has won a medal in judo in every Olympic games since 1972, indeed that was the first year that the judo was accepted on the main programme. Barcelona also saw the introduction of women's judo for the first time.

What the British team have never done, is win gold. There was considerable optimism in the British camp, as we have produced a string of world and European champions in recent years, but alas, in the end, four medals came our way, two silver, two bronze but no gold. A total of four medals, when

there were just 14 competitors, meant that the judo squad were to return from Barcelona as one of the most successful, despite the frustration of not winning gold. " Under the conditions, the performance of the team was magnificent," declared British Judo Association chairman, George Kerr.

Of all the medals that the British team took home, none was more unexpected than the one taken by Ray Stevens in the half-heavyweight section. Ray is a superb technician, but is not known a man who can get tough. He relied on his skill, until he came up against the eventu-

al gold medallist, Antal Kovacs from Hungary. In the end, Stevens' lighter frame told.

Inspired by Ray Stevens' performance, Kate Howey took the bronze in the women's middleweight section. She lost on the judges' decision to the Cuban, Odalis Reve Jimenez.

Nicola Fairbrother, the other silver medallist, had a tough time competing in front of the 6,000 spectators. But Nicola, a sports journalist from Surrey, bore the pressure with composure and fought splendidly. But the Spanish favourite, Miriam Blasco, probably the greatest female

Udo Quellmalz comes to the rescue with a bronze. He was Germany's only medal winner in the judo.

Success and failure. Alexandra Schreiber lost her bout against Heidi Rakels (far left). Philippe Tayot won the silver in the middleweight section.

Hungarian Antal Kovacs takes the gold against Ray Stevens, the first British judo medallist in Barcelona (far left). Frank Moreño Garcia struggles with David Douillet, one of the seven French judo medal-winners.

119

A gesture of gratitude. Korean judoka, Mi-Jung Kim, celebrates after winning the gold in the half-heavyweight section.

Victoire. Catherine Fleury took the gold in the 61kg category, one of the two French golds in judo.

judoka in the world, was magnificent and Nicola had no complaints about the final outcome.

One contest left a bad taste in the mouth. In one of the semi-finals for the women's featherweight section, despite the evident superiority of Sharon Rendle and the frequency of her attacks, the two judges appeared to be swayed by the vociferous support of the 6,000-strong audience. They then gave the fight to the local favourite Almuneda Muñoz. Even one of the Spanish black belts remarked that he was embarrassed. "That was not judo." George Kerr was not a happy man. "I must say that it was the refereeing that deprived Sharon Rendle of an almost certain gold. It was atrocious." Not normally one for whingeing, Kerr made his feelings known to the authorities. He wanted to make it clear that he didn't want a reversal of the decision, but he wanted to prevent a repetition of what he felt was biased refereeing.

Karen Briggs, four times champion in her category, was probably the worst victim of misfortune. She had to be sedated in a Barcelona hospital, when, after dislocating her shoulder, she tried to put it back into joint. It was no surprise when she was eliminated by the 16 year-old Japanese, Ryoko Tamura.

While Karen has probably said goodbye to further Olympic opportunities, Nicola Fairbrother, at 22, will be setting her sights on Atlanta and maybe that elusive British gold will be hers.

Floored by defeat, the German, Stefan Dott came fifth in his category. The German team gave a disappointing performance.

Smiling Catherine Fleury shows off her gold medal. The French judoka won the half-middle-weight category.

A friendly gesture after a tough fight. Udo Quellmatz consoles the defeated Belgian Gaston.

Tears of emotion on the podium. French judo star, Cecile Nowak, took the top prize in the super-lightweight category.

WOMEN

- 48 kg

Extra-lightweight   02.08.1992

1. C. Nowak (FRA)
2. R. Tamura (JPN)
3. H. Senyurt (TUR)
3. A. Savon Carmenaty (CUB)

- 52 kg

Half-lightweight   01.08.1992

1. A. Muñoz Martinez (ESP)
2. N. Mizoguchi (JPN)
3. Z. Li (CHN)
3. S.S. Rendle (GBR)

- 56 kg

Lightweight   31.07.1992

1. M. Blasco Soto (ESP)
2. N.K. Fairbrother (GBR)
3. C. Tateno (JPN)
3. D. Gonzales Morales (CUB)

5. N. Flagothier (BEL)
5. K.M. Donahoo (USA)
7. C. Arnaud (FRA)

- 61 kg

Half-middleweight   30.07.1992

1. C. Fleury (FRA)
2. Y. Arad (ISR)
3. D. Zhang (CHN)
3. E. Petrova (EUN)

- 66 kg

Middleweight   29.07.1992

1. O. Reve Jimenez (CUB)
2. E. Pierantozzi (ITA)
3. H. Rakels (BEL)
3. K. L. Howey (GBR)

- 72 kg

Half-middleweight   28.07.1992

1. Mi-Jung Kim (KOR)
2. Y. Tanabe (JPN)
3. I. de Kok (NED)
3. L. Meignan (FRA)

+ 72 kg

Heavyweight   27.07.1992

1. X. Zhuang (CHN)
2. E. Rodriguez Villanueva (CUB)
3. N. Lupino (FRA)
3. Y. Sakaue (JPN)

MEN

- 60 kg

Extra-lightweight   02.08.1992

1. N. Gousseinov (EUN)
2. Hyun Yoon (KOR)
3. T. Koshino (JPN)
3. R. Trautmann (GER)

5. J. Wagner (HUN)
5. P. Pradayrol (FRA)
7. W. B. Garcia Garcia (VEN)
7. D. Battulga (MGL)

- 65 kg

Half-lightweight   01.08.1992

1. R. Sampaio Cardoso (BRA)
2. J. Csak (HUN)
3. U. G. Quellmalz (GER)
3. I. Hernandez Planas (CUB)

5. P. Laats (BEL)
5. F. Lorenzo Aparicio (ESP)
7. K. Maruyama (JPN)
7. Sang-Moon Kim (KOR)

- 71 kg

Lightweight   31.07.1992

1. T. Koga (JPN)
2. B. Hajtos (HUN)
3. Hoon Chung (KOR)
3. S. O. Smadga (ISR)
5. B. Carabetta (FRA)
5. S. Dott (GER)
7. W. Blach (POL)
7. K. Boldbaatar (MGL)

- 78 kg

Half-middleweight   30.07.1992

1. H. Yoshida (JPN)
2. J. Morris (USA)
3. B. Damaisin (FRA)
3. Byung-Joo Kim (KOR)

5. J. Laats (BEL)
5. L. Adolfsson (SWE)

- 86 kg

Middleweight   29.07.1992

1. W. Legien (POL)
2. P. Tayot (FRA)
3. H. Okada (JPN)
3. N. Gill (CAN)

5. A. Croitoru (ROM)
5. A. Lobenstein (GER)

- 95 kg

Half-heavyweight   28.07.1992

1. A. Kovacs (HUN)
2. R. Stevens (GBR)
3. D. Sergeev (EUN)
3. T. Meijer (NED)

5. P. Nastula (POL)
5. I. Pertelson (EST)

+ 95 kg

Heavyweight   27.07.1992

1. D. Khakhaleichvili (EUN)
2. N. Ogawa (JPN)
3. D. Douillet (FRA)
3. I. Czosz (HUN)

5. F. Moreno Garcia (CUB)
5. H. van Barneveld (BEL)
7. E. Perez Lobo (ESP)

Turkey's tabloid hero is twice the top man

Not many of us were around the last time Britain won an Olympic gold medal at weightlifting. It was in 1896, the first games of the modern era. To count British successes since then, you only need the fingers of one hand. The last success was in 1984 in Los Angeles, when David Mercer took the bronze. British reputations have not been enhanced by the sad affair of Andrew Davies and Andrew Saxton. Both young men were expelled for alleged drug abuse in the first few days of the Games.

Memories of Seoul

There were fears that there might be a repeat of the events in Seoul. The whole of the Bulgarian weightlifting team walked out after several of their members had tested positive. Olympic officials feared that this sport, which is high on grunts and groans, was also high on other stimulants. However, in this Olympiad, weightlifting has retrieved some of its dignity, even if it still remains on the IOC's 'hit list' of sports under scrutiny for the future because of the crowded Olympic timetable.

A virtuoso performance from the South Korean, Chun Byung-Kwan, brought his country its first Olympic title in the bantamweight. The Korean's close challenger, Liu Shou-bin from China, came to a halt at 147.5 kg. Chun then went for the world record, lifting 170 kg, a total

which would have made him only the second man in history to lift more than three times his own weight. He got the bar as far as his shoulders and there it stopped. The Russians, or rather the Unified Team maintained their dominance of the event and an analysis of the results reveals that they won five out of the ten categories. Georgian Kakhi Kakhiachvili set a new world record in the middle-heavyweight class.

Turkish delight

The 25-year-old Turk, Naim-Suleymanoglu, is pound-for-pound the strongest weightlifter in the world and said to be the greatest of all time. At the age of 15, he had attained his first world record and went on to hold the world record in three categories - snatch, clean and jerk in the 60kg division - but he has not been in top form recently. In the final, the tiny Turk showed his mettle by easily beating his main challenger, the Bulgarian, Nikolai Peshalov. Suleymanoglu assumed god-like status in Turkey after winning gold at Seoul. The Turks have a rare sense of national pride in Suleymanoglu and it is said that he returned from Seoul in the prime minister's private jet. But he had recently declared himself bored with the sport - and with the ever-increasing demands to win titles and break world records. The Bulgarian's strong performances provided the

"Everyone wants to be the strongest in the world," said Manfred Neuburger (bronze, left). But that turned out to be Germany's Ronny Weller (gold, above).

That's what happens, when it really is too much. Udo Guse (above) is a heavyweight, but not a medal winner.

He could try the high jump as well. Pole Waldemar Malak is overjoyed having won the bronze medal in the heavyweight division.

Turk with the necessary motivation, which is clearly getting harder to find. A millionaire at 21 and apparently enjoying the front page headlines about his private life, he obviously felt that retirement at 24 might leave an unfillable gap in his life.

Bronze medal hits the deck

The weightlifting event has often brought with it some emotionally-charged moments and it was left to the Russian, Ibrahim Samadov, to give the Olympic authorities a headache. Disappointed at coming only third in the light-heavyweight division, he threw down his bronze medal in disgust. The considered response of the IOC was to ban Samadov for life and he was relieved of his medal. The Unified Team claimed that Samadov had merely dropped the medal because 'he felt faint'.

Down but not out

Another emotional moment came when the German Ronny Weller mounted the podium to collect his gold medal. Two and a half years ago, he had been lying in hospital in a coma after a road accident in which his girlfriend, Sylvia, lost her life. He too suffered a broken skull and numerous other fractures and yet, after months of orthopaedic surgery, the man who came third in Seoul and who was once down but not out, mounted the podium to cheers from his fans. In tears, he told them: "I did it for Sylvia."

Kakhi Kakhiachvili, winner of the middle-heavyweight division, proved that, despite the political changes, the eastern Europeans are still masters in the weight-lifting.

Andreas Behm (above) believes that there is no need for drugs. He took the bronze medal in the lightweight category.

Clearly not satisfied with his performance is Yong Wang. This Chinese civil servant would not have been satisfied with his final ranking either. He came tenth.

Viktor Tregoubov (above) is a winner in one of the hea-vyweight classes. Another gold for Naim Suleymanoglu (top). He has become a Turkish folk hero and was bidding to retain his feather-weight title.

- 90 kg

Middle-heavyweight	01.08.1992
1. K. Kakhiachvili (EUN)	412.5
2. S. Syrtsov (EUN)	412.5
3. S. Wolczaniecki (POL)	392.5
4. Byung-Chan Kim (KOR)	380.0
5. I. Tchakarov (BUL)	377.5
6. E. Lara Rodriguez (CUB)	375.0

- 67.5 kg

Lightweight	29.07.1992
1. I. Militossian (EUN)	337.5
2. Y. V. Yotov (BUL)	327.5
3. A. Brehm (GER)	320.0
4. A. Yahlaoui (ALG)	315.0
5. J. J. Gronman (FIN)	305.0
6. E. Acevedo Tabares (COL)	300.0
7. Sang Ho Im (PRK)	300.0
8. P. Bushi (ALB)	290.0

- 100 kg

100 Kilogram	02.08.1992
1. V. Tregoubov (EUN)	410.0
2. T. Taimazov (EUN)	402.5
3. W. Malak (POL)	400.0
4. F. Tournefier (FRA)	387.5
5. P. I. Stefanov (BUL)	380.0
6. A. Danisov (ISR)	377255

- 56 kg

Bantamweight	27.07.1992
1. Byung-Kwan Chun (KOR)	287.5
2. S. Liu (CHN)	277.5
3. J. Luo (CHN)	277.5
4. L. Fombertasse (FRA)	260.0
5. K. Sakuma (JPN)	255.0
6. T. Karczag (HUN)	255.0
7. Yong Chol Kim (PRK)	255.0
8. M. Gorzelniak (POL)	255.0

- 75 kg

Middleweight	30.07.1992
1. F. Kassapu (EUN)	357.5
2. P. Lara Rodriguez (CUB)	357.5
3. Myong Nam Kim (PRK)	352.5
4. A. Kozlowski (POL)	352.5
5. I. Steinhöfel (GER)	347.5
7. W. Chlebosz (POL)	340.0
8. G. Lu (CHN)	335.0
16. O. Caruso (GER)	325.0

- 110 kg

Heavyweight	03.08.1992
1. R. Weller (GER)	432.5
2. A. Akoev (EUN)	430.0
3. S. Botev (BUL)	417.5
4. N. Vlad (ROM)	405.0
5. F. Seipelt (GER)	390.0
6. P. Saltsidis (GRE)	385.0

- 52 kg

Flyweight	26.07.1992
1. I. Ivanov (BUL)	265.0
2. Q. Lin (CHN)	262.5
3. T. Giharean (ROM)	252.5
4. Kwang-Ku Ko (KOR)	252.5
5. H. Mutlu (TUR)	247.5
6. Nam Su Gil (PRK)	235.0
7. H. Fuentes Rodriguez (VEN)	230.0
8. J. A. Ibañez Puig (ESP)	227.5
9. A. Irei (JPN)	222.5

- 60 kg

Featherweight	28.07.1992
1. N. Suleymanoglu (TUR)	320.0
2. N. Peshalov (BUL)	305.0
3. Y. He (CHN)	295.0
4. N. S. Terziiski (BUL)	295.0
5. V. Leonidis (GRE)	295.0
6. Hyon Il Ro (PRK)	287.5
7. A. Czanka (HUN)	285.0
8. Jae Son Li (PRK)	280.0

- 82.5 kg

Light-heavyweight	31.07.1992
1. P. Dimas (GRE)	370.0
2. K. Siemion (POL)	370.0
3. I. Samadov (EUN) disqualified	370.0
4. Chol Ho Chon (PRK)	365.0
5. P. I. Bratoitchev (BUL)	365.0
6. L. E. Elias Ocaña (CUB)	365.0

+ 110 kg

Super-heavyweight	04.08.1992
1. A. Kourlovitch (EUN)	245.0
2. L. Aranenko (EUN)	237.5
3. M. Nerlinger (GER)	232.5
4. E. Aguero Shell (CUB)	230.0
5. J. Zubricky (TCH)	222.5
6. E. Arslan (TUR)	220.0
7. M. Zawieja (GER)	210.0

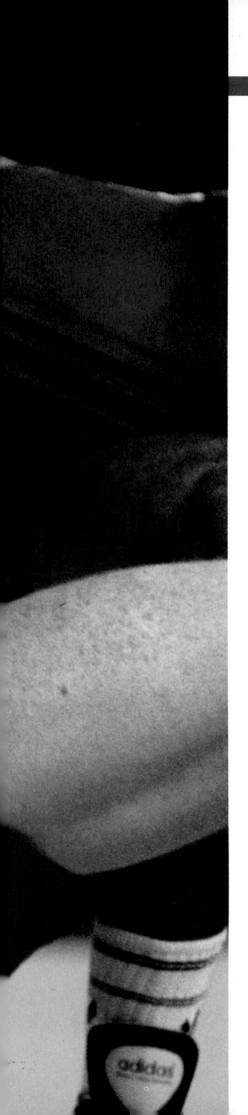

The art of wrestling

A return to attractive wrestling had been promised. The sport, perhaps the original form of man-to-man combat, had clearly degenerated in recent years, characterized by delaying tactics and the fear of losing. In time for the Olympic Games, the International Amateur Wrestling Federation (FILA) had introduced a rule change which allowed referees to penalize passive fighters. Activity and creativity were to be rewarded, not just thwarting an opponent's attacks. FILA's president, Milan Ercegan, made a telling comparison: "Wrestling is movement. Negative tactics must be punished. That applies to wrestlers as well as coaches. In gymnastics, no one would get top marks just for sitting on top of the pommel horse." So a decision in the interest of the spectators! But within the wrestling fraternity it was controversial. The reason became clear enough in the early bouts. Referees were no longer impressed with the big names, established rankings were upset. Many favourites bit the dust in the early rounds of the Graeco-Roman tournament. They included Raúl Martinéz Alemán, the Cuban world champion in the 52-kg division, and Sergej Demiashkievich, the twice world champion from the Commonwealth of Independent States in the 100-kg division. Three reigning Olympic champions, Andrzej Wronski (Poland), Aranas Komshev (Bulgaria) and Norbert Novenyi (Hungary), also squandered their chances of repeating their wins at Seoul in 1988. Then they had competed in different weight divisions, now they all fought in the heavyweight division and made life difficult for each other.

The Russian Aleksandr Karolin, who won in the super-heavyweight division, added yet another success to an unprecedented series. At 1.96 metres tall and weighing 128 kg, he is not an easy man to throw. A powerhouse who by no means relies just on the strength of his tree-trunk legs, the 24-year-old had been unbeaten since March 1988. He had adjusted to the new passivity rule. With a few well-executed

Swedish wrestler, Torbjörn Kornbakk beat Cuban, Nestor Almanza, to win the bronze.

Down and out. Alexander Ignatenko (left) needs a hand to get back on his feet.

grips, he gained his second Olympic gold.

The German, Maik Bullmann, won a gold with a similarly convincing display. His 5-0 defeat of Hakki Basar of Turkey in the final of the 90-kg division was particularly impressive. The world champion made a name for himself on the mat with his attacking style. Ninety minutes before his bout, his team mate, Rifat Yildiz, had lost to South Korea's Han-bong 6-5 in extra time after a highly controversial decision and despite having led 5-2 in regular time. Whenever sporting success is determined by subjective judgements, favouritism is always a possibility.

Nowhere did this manifest itself more flagrantly than in the final of the 82-kg division. The superior Elmadi Yabrailov from the Unified Team was refused a score in regular time, and the American Kevin Jackson then proceeded to win 1-0 in extra time. Deeply upset and in tears, Zhabraizhiov had to be virtually dragged to the medal ceremony by his coach, but he would not let the official put the silver medal around his neck. Although cheated of this gold medal, the Unified Team from the Commonwealth of Independent States was still the most successful, as the Soviet Union had been in previous Olympics, with 16 medals (six gold, five silver, five bronze). Traditionally–strong wrestling countries like Hungary, Sweden and Romania did not figure. Americans and Koreans have taken their place. Times are indeed a-changing in the wrestling world.

Maik, the new Hercules

Maik Bullmann, the German wrestler was born in 1967. Michael was one of the commonest names for German boys. Maik's parents would like to have called him 'Mike' but they had a problem. They lived in Frankfurt, not Frankfurt on Main, Germany's commercial capital located in the heart of Europe, but Frankfurt on the Oder. This Frankfurt is a forgotten little town in eastern Germany, which sits astride the German-Polish border. The problem for Maik's parents was that, at the time of his birth, Frankfurt on the Oder was in the German Democratic Republic, well behind the Iron Curtain, and in those days still rigidly patrolled by the Soviet army. To have called their son Mike, an American-sounding name, would have been misconstrued by the Communist authorities. Only Maik's parents can say why they chose this unorthodox spelling, but one thing is certain: Maik started out as favourite in the light-heavyweight wrestling competition and he became the champion by beating the Turk, Hakki Basar. Bullmann disposed of all of his opponents with consummate ease. He moved his heavy muscular body with amazing speed and deployed enormous strength....a veritable Hercules. But how did his parents hit on the name Maik? It is not listed in any register of names anywhere in the world. The Bullman's gold medal winning son runs a pub in Frankfurt am Oder. It's called 'Bulles Café'. One thing is certain: his customers will know that they had better behave themselves.

The South Korean bantamweight, Han-Bong An, revels in victory.

A furious battle between Leri Khabelov (EUN) and Heiko Balz (GER) before Khabelov took the gold.

GRECO-ROMAN

"Now then, shake hands" - Hector Milian (CUB) having just beaten the American, Dennis Koslowski.

- 48 kg

Light-flyweight	29.07.1992

1. O. Koutcherenko (EUN)
2. V. Maenza (ITA)
3. W. Sanchez (CUB)
4. F. Yildiz (GER)
5. I. Dascalescu (ROM)
6. R. Simkhah (IRI)

- 52 kg

Flyweight	28.07.1992

1. J. Rönningen (NOR)
2. A. Ter-Mkrtytchan (EUN)
3. Kap Min Kyung (KOR)
4. S. Sheldon (USA)
5. B. T. Tzenov (BUL)
6. V. Rebegea (ROM)

- 57 kg

Bantamweight	30.07.1992

1. Han-Bong An (KOR)
2. R. Yildiz (GER)
3. Z. Sheng (CHN)
4. A. Ignatenko (EUN)
5. W. Lara (CUB)
6. M. Sandu (ROM)
7. K. Pehkonen (FIN)
8. D. Hall (USA)
9. A. Naanaa (MAR)

- 62 kg

Featherweight	30.07.1992

1. M. Akif Pirim (TUR)
2. S. Martynov (EUN)
3. J. Maren (CUB)
4. W. Zawadzki (POL)
5 J. Bodi (HUN)
6. A. Lee (USA)

- 68 kg

Lightweight	28.07.1992

1. A. Repka (HUN)
2. I. Dougoutchiev (EUN)
3. R. S. Smith (USA)
4. C. E. Perez Rodriguez (CUB)
5. G. Yalouz (FRA)
6. A. Chamangolz (IRI)

- 74 kg

Welterweight	29.07.1992

1. M. Iskandarian (EUN)
2. J. Tracz (POL)
3. T. Kornbakk (SWE)
4. N. Almanza (CUB)
5. Y. Riemer (FRA)
6. A. Marchl (AUT)

- 82 kg

Middleweight	30.07.1992

1. P. Farkas (HUN)
2. P. Stepien (POL)
3. D. Tourlykhanov (EUN)
4. M. Fredriksson (SWE)
5. T. Niemi (FIN)
6. G. Kasum (IOP)

- 90 kg

Light-heavyweight	30.07.1992

1. M. Bullmann (GER)
2. H. Basar (TUR)
3. G. Kogouachvili (EUN)
4. M. Ljungberg (SWE)
5. H. Babak (IRI)
6. M. Foy (USA)
7. R. Peña (CUB)
8. S. Campanella (ITA)
9. F. Marx (AUT)

- 100 kg

Heavyweight	28.07.1992

1. H. Milian (CUB)
2. D. Koslowski (USA)
3. S. Demiashkievitch (EUN)
4. A. Wronski (POL)
5. A. Steinbach (GER)
6. I. Ieremciuc (ROM)

+ 100 kg

Super-heavy	29.07.1992

1. A. Kareline (EUN)
2. T. Johansson (SWE)
3. I. Grigoras (ROM)
4. L. Klauz (HUN)
5. A. Borodow (CAN)
6. L. Tian (CHN)

No modest understatement here: Alejandro Puerto (CUB) is absolutely delighted about his gold medal.

Forgotten something? At least it made no difference to Bullmann's victory (above).

Maik Bullmann swept all before him to take the first German gold in wrestling.

FREESTYLE

- 48 kg
Light-flyweight	06.08.1992
1. Il Kim (PRK)	
2. Jong Kim (KOR)	
3. V. Oroudjov (EUN)	
4. R. Rasovan (ROM)	
5. T. Vanni (USA)	
6. R. Heugabel (GER)	
7. A. Martinez (CUB)	
8. T. Khosbayar (MGL)	
9. T. Petryshen (CAN)	

- 52 kg
Flyweight	05.08.1992
1. Hak Li (PRK)	
2. JR. Jones (USA)	
3. V. Jordanov (BUL)	
4. Sun Kim (KOR)	
5. A. Orel (TUR)	
6. M. Sato (JPN)	

- 57 kg
Bantamweight	07.08.1992
1. A. Puerto (CUB)	
2. S. Smal (EUN)	
3. Yong Sik Kim (PRK)	
4. R. Musaoglu (TUR)	
5. R. Pavlov (BUL)	
6. K. Cross (USA)	
7. J. Scheibe (GER)	
8. R. Dawson (CAN)	

- 62 kg
Featherweight	07.08.1992
1. J. Smith (USA)	
2. A. Mohammedian (IRI)	
3. L. Reinoso Martinez (CUB)	
4. R. M. Vassiliev (BUL)	
5. M. Azizov (EUN)	
6. M. Ilhan (AUS)	

- 68 kg
Lightweight	05.08.1992
1. A. Fadzaev (EUN)	
2. V. Getzov (BUL)	
3. K. Akaishi (JPN)	
4. A. Akbarnejad (IRI)	
5. F. Ozbas (TUR)	
6. Young Ko (KOR)	

- 74 kg
Welterweight	06.08.1992
1. J. Park (KOR)	
2. K. Monday (USA)	
3. A.Khadem (IRI)	
4. M. Gadjiev (EUN)	
5. K. Walencik (POL)	
6. G. Holmes (CAN)	

- 82 kg
Middleweight	07.08.1992
1. K. Jackson (USA)	
2. E. Dschabrailov (EUN)	
3. R. Khadem (IRI)	
4. H. Gstöttner (GER)	
5. J. Lohyna (TCH)	
6. S. Öztürk (TUR)	

- 90 kg
Light-heavyweight	07.08.1992
1. M. Khadartsev (EUN)	
2. K. Simsek (TUR)	
3. C. Campbell (USA)	
4. P. Sukhbat (MGL)	
5. A. Bani (IRI)	
6. R. Limonta (CUB)	

- 100 kg
Heavyweight	05.08.1992
1. L. Khabelov (EUN)	
2. H. Balz (GER)	
3. A. Kayali (TUR)	
4. Tae Kim (KOR)	
5. A. Radomski (POL)	
6. S. Verma (IND)	

+ 100 kg
Super-heavy	06.08.1992
1. B. Baumgartner (USA)	
2. J. Thue (CAN)	
3. D. Gobedjichvili (EUN)	
4. M. Demir (TUR)	
5. A. Schröder (GER)	
6. A. Karbalai (IRI)	
7. C. Wang (CHN)	
8. Sung Park (KOR)	

Runcorn's Robin brings back a bronze

When Robin Reid beat Norway's Ole Klemetsen in their light-middle-weight quarter final bout, it became certain that he would win at least a bronze medal. But boxing as an Olympic sport was on trial in Barcelona. The risk of head injury in boxing has become a burning issue and the severe injuries suffered by a British boxer has brought the matter into closer focus. A British neuropathologist, Dr Helen Grant, has been commissioned to write a report for the IOC on the danger of suffering brain damage in the ring and there is a strong possibility that boxing will be off the Olympic agenda by 1996, though Reid will be hoping otherwise. The 21-year-old bookmaker's cashier from Runcorn started to look forward to a money-spinning professional career. "I have professional ambitions and people have made offers. But there will be plenty of time for that when I get home." Reid had made meticulous preparations for the semi-final, in which he was to meet Dutchman Orhan Delibas. Time was spent studying tapes of the man who might bar his way to the finals and the top medal. He lost on points to Delibas in the Olympic qualifying tournament last March. "He is a small, stocky fighter who is in and out all the time. We'll be working on the tactics needed to cope with him." But it was not enough. Reid looked lacklustre throughout the three rounds and

was beaten 8-3 on points. He could have no complaints about the result, although he had caused a few problems for his opponent in the second round. "He was too slippy, very elusive, but it's still bronze - I wanted to go through to the final but that's the way it goes." It turned out to be Britain's only boxing medal. Irish boxer, Michael Carruth, however, gave his supporters and fellow countrymen something to celebrate. In the welterweight class, Ireland won their first gold medal of any kind since 1956. As he stood on the podium and the Irish anthem played, a bystander remarked: "That's a sound he'll remember for the rest of his life." Carruth's determination and intelligence outwitted the tall

Gold for the German: German Boxer, Andreas Tews beat 17-year-old Spanish fighter, Faustino Reyes in the featherweight category.

Jan Quast, a half-heavyweight, lost his semi-final fight, but both losing semi-finalists win a bronze (below).

The Cubans won seven out of 12 gold medals in the boxing. Below: Joel Cassamayor in the bantamweight.

The other German boxing finalist was Marco Rudolph. He won all his earlier fights convincingly (above).

Cuban, Juan Hernandez. Michael and his father, Austin, one of the Irish coaches, had devised a plan to unsettle the Cuban. "They aren't as effective as when they have to come forward. The idea was to make him come at me." Carruth, a triplet from south Dublin, went into the final round level on 8-8. Practically, every member of the Irish Olympic team was there and Carruth did not disappoint them, coming in as the winner at 13-10. The Irish brigade could not control themselves. Michael leapt into the air and then bounded around the ring. "It was such a great thrill," he said. The Irish medal tally had been boosted a little earlier, when the Cubans had turned the tables on Irishman, Wayne McCullough. The Cuban, Joel Casamajor, outpointed him in the bantamweight final, but McCullough was thrilled by his silver medal. He had fought bravely and won the final round on points, but a poor start had put him in irretrievable situation. The Americans had a poor tournament, with only two finalists. Elsewhere the boxing, predictably, proved to be of great benefit to the Cuban gold reserves. The team won seven out the 12 boxing finals. Two Britons reached the quarter-finals but Steve Wilson and Peter Richardson both ultimately succumbed to stronger east European opponents.

RESULTS

The hopes of the American boxers came to nothing. In the middleweight class, Chris Byrd lost to Ariel Hernandez.

At last it's mine! Torsten May, half-heavyweight from Frankfurt on the Oder was already the world champion, but this medal counts just as much.

Andreas Tews receives some advice from his corner (top). The Cubans were almost invincible (above).

- 54 kg

Bantamweight 08.08.1992

1. J. Casamayor (CUB)
2. W. McCullough (IRL)
3. M. Achik (MAR)
3. Gwang Li (PRK)
5. R. Molina (ARG)
5. S. Todorov (BUL)

- 57 kg

Featherweight 09.08.1992

1. A. Tews (GER)
2. F. Reyes (ESP)
3. H. Soltani (ALG)
3. R. Paliani (EUN)
5. E. Suarez (CUB)
5. V. Damien (DOM)
5. Duk Park (KOR)
5. D. Dumitrescu (ROM)

- 48 kg

Light-flyweight 08.08.1992

1. R. Marcelo (CUB)
2. D. Bojinov (BUL)
3. J. Quast (GER
3. R. Velasco (PHI)
5. R. Lozano (ESP)
5. R. Williams (GBR)

- 51 kg

Flyweight 09.08.1992

1. Chol Choi (PRK)
2. R. Gonzales (CUB)
3. I. Kovacs (HUN)
3. T. Austin (USA)
5. R. Peden (AUS)
5. H. Avila (DOM)

- 60 kg

Lightweight 08.08.1992

1. O. De la Hoya (USA)
2. M. Rudolph (GER)
3. Sung Hong (KOR)
3. N. Bayarsaikhan (MGL)
5. D. Tontchev (MGL)
5. J. Lorcy (BUL)

- 63,5 kg

Light-welterweight 09.08.1992

1. H. Vinent (CUB)
2. M. Ludec (CAN)
3. J. Kjall (FIN)
3. L. Doroftei (ROM)
5. L. Bouneb (ALG)
5. O. Nikolaev (EUN)
5. P. Richardson (GBR)
5. Laszlo Szucs (HUN)

- 67 kg

Welterweight 08.08.1992

1. M. Carruth (IRL)
2. J. Hernandez (CUB)
3. A. Acevedo (PUR)
3. A. Chenglai (THA)
5. A. Otto (GER)
5. Karpaciauskas (LIT)
5. F. Vastag (ROM)
5. S. Antman (SWE)

- 71 kg

Light-middleweight 09.08.1992

1. J. Lemus (CUB)
2. O. Delibars (NED)
3. R. Reid (GBR)
3. G. Mizsei (HUN)
5. F. Maselino (ASA)
5. I. Saplavskis (LAT)
5. O. Klemetsen (NOR)
5. R. Marquez (USA)

- 75 kg

Middleweight 08.08.1992

1. A. Hernandez (CUB)
2. C. C. Byrd (USA)
3. C. Johnson (CAN)
3. Seung Lee (KOR)
5. A. Dine (ALG)
5. S. Trendafilov (BUL)
5. S. Ottke (GER)

- 81 kg

Light-heavyweight 09.08.1992

1. T. May (GER)
2. R. Zaoúlitchnyi (EUN)
3. Z. Beres (HUN)
3. W. Bartnik (POL)

- 91 kg

Heavyweight 08.08.1992

1. S. Felix (CUB)
2. D. Izonritel (NGR)
3. van der Lijde (NED)
3. D. Tua (NZL)
5. K. Johnson (CAN)
5. P. Douglas (IRL)

+ 91 kg

Super-heavyweight 09.08.1992

1. R. Balado (CUB)
2. R. Igbinegha (NGR)
3. S. Roussinov (BUL)
3. B. Nielsen (DEN)
5. W. Fischer (GER)
5. G. Juskevicius (LIT)
5 P. Hrivnak (TCH)
5 L. Donald (USA)

Newcomers to a traditional preserve

Giovanna Trillini, the gold medallist in the women's foil, easily the star of this summer's fencing competition (far left).

Fencing, like archery and javelin throwing, grew out of warfare. The first iron swords can be traced back as far as 1000 BC, although at the time they were used for stabbing rather than for the kind of fine point play we know today.

To develop fencing for its own sake, practice was needed rather than simply the bumping off of fellow warriors. And so a form of fencing had to be devised with rules to prevent injury. The next significant step came with the development of tempered steel in the 16th century. At around this time, firearms had already overtaken the sword as the best way of killing people. The sword developed into the light, thin and elegant weapon of choice for gentlemen to avenge slights. (However, contrary to myth and Hollywood, duels were usually decided by first blood rather than death). The precursor of today's rules of fencing developed in the 18th century, and it became a natural sport for the first Olympics in 1896. Since that time, it has been one of six omnipresent sports. In recent years, however, there has been talk, much to the alarm of the fencing establishment, of reducing the number of weapons and contests at Olympic level in favour of sports more readily understandable to the novice spectator.

Fatalities

Thankfully, one of the most common concerns on the part of spectators new to the sport, namely that one of the participants could be injured, is rarely justified. Probably the best-known victim is Vladimir Smirnov from the former Soviet Union, who won the gold in Moscow in 1980. Two years later at the world cham-

Gold medals for the five musketeers from the German "medal factory": Ulrich Schreck, Alexander Koch, Thorsten Weidner, Udo Wanger and Ingo Weissenborn.

After failing to win a single medal in the individual competitions, the Germans came up trumps in the team sports, here beating the Cubans to the gold.

In the women's individual foil, the Germans felt the lack of Anja Fichtel. Sabine Bau, who came seventh, was their best performer (left).

pionships, the foil of his opponent broke and pierced his eye through the mask. Smirnov died nine days later.

The Rules

Fencing is divided into three weapons as follows: the foil, based on the original training weapon for gentlemen's swordfights; the épée, based on the genuine duelling sword and practically indistinguishable from the foil; and finally the sabre, based on the slashing action of a cavalryman's sword rather than the piercing qualities of the other two weapons. Of the three weapons, the épée is said to be the easiest to learn. It is heavier than the foil or sabre, the whole body is the target area and every hit counts. This means that simultaneous hits count against both players. Given this potential vulnerability, most épée contests are battles of patience as well as skill. In the foil and sabre, where only the upper part of the body forms the target area and a hit has to follow set movements (attack, riposte and counter-riposte), competitors tend to be more aggressive in their approach. Hits must be made with the point in foil and épée. In sabre, the cutting edge also counts, as does the first third of the upper edge of the blade.

The Rulers

The strongest fencing nations are France, Germany, Italy and the CIS. Indeed up until quite recently, the sport was dominated at an Olympic level by three nations: France, Italy and Hungary. Even after Barcelona, hopes of a fencing medal for Britain continue to remain unrealised. Britain won their only fencing gold medal through Gilian Shee in the women's foil in Melbourne in 1956 when Alan Jay won the silver in the men's foil, but have won no medals of any hue ever since Bill Hoskyns took the silver in the men's épée in Tokyo in 1964. And yet this year Britain came closer than ever. Fiona McCarthy, the 31 year-old from Edinburgh, got into the last eight in

the final of the women's foil, to the visible delight of her team mates.

The Old Rivalry

Barcelona in 1992 was only the latest instalment in the continuing saga of rivalry between the Hungarians and the Italians. Perhaps its origins are to be found in an incident during the 1924 Olympics, when the Hungarian fencing judge, Kovacs, became so involved in an argument with an Italian fencer, Aldo Boni, that the matter escalated into a duel four weeks later between the son of the Hungarian coach and the Italian captain. Kovacs' relations with the Italians did not improve with the sabre competition of that year. On that occasion, he quarrelled with the Italian Oreste Puliti, which in turn led to another post-Olympic duel. This time it was Kovacs himself who had to fight – against Puliti on the Hungarian-Yugoslav border. The two men fought for two hours before spectators, worried about the harm they were doing each other, called a halt to the fight. History does not record whether Kovacs returned as a judge in the Games in '28.

Sabre

This year, in the individual sabre competition, the Italo-Hungarian question again came to the fore, but was resolved in the traditional manner as far as sabre was concerned, by the Hungarian Bence Szabo taking the gold medal and the Italian man, Marco Marin, the silver.

Bence Szabo rejoices at his gold (below). Anja Fichtel, master fencer and mother in one, was the key to victory for the German women's team (bottom).

Men´s Foil and Épée

In foil and épée, the French and Italians have shared domination over the years. The most extraordinary performance in Olympic fencing must be that of the Italian, Nedo Nadi, who embraced all three disciplines. In 1920, he won the individual title in both foil and sabre and shared in the team title for all three weapons. In the épée at least, Nadi´s countrymen were left empty-handed this year in Barcelona. thanks to the efforts of the Frenchmen, Eric Srecki and Jean-Michel Henry, who took the men´s individual gold and bronze medals for épée, with the Russian Pavel Kolobkov taking the silver. In the foil, two men who know each other well fought it out for gold and silver. The sight of Sergei Golubtski (CIS) and Philippe Omnes (France) shaking hands and smiling at each other encouragingly was a genuinely happy moment of pure sportsmanship. In the end, Omnes took the gold and Golubtski silver.

Women´s foil

But when it came to the women´s foil final, the lack of Italian gold medals up to that point was more than made good by Italy providing the star of this summer´s competition - Giovanna Trillini. In Olympic fencing, women are still struggling to win equal rights (women only being allowed to compete in one weapon, foil, against the men´s three at Olympic level). Outnumbered they may be, but the women certainly provided plenty of interest in the shape of Trillini, possibly the most charismatic and exciting fencer at the Games. Trillini took a gold at the 1991 World Championships and managed to do the same in Barcelona in the individual competition. This was at the expense of some considerable display of German emotion, Sabine Bau sobbing openly in the quarter finals as she lost to Trillini. In both of the bouts there, Bau had been in the lead 3:0 at first, only to leave the piste after losing to the Italian woman. The other hopes in Germany´s

Once-confident victors in the 'Slough of Despond'

German fencers have for years been seen as sure-fire medal winners. And since it does add to one´s sense of self-worth to have been the assured national supplier of such honours over a period of years, the slightest criticism can be hard to bear. This year, the German fencers had to go without medals for nearly a week in the Games - after which point the criticism at home was beginning to turn from disappointment into gloating. Of course this is the price to be paid by any standard-bearer of national pride - even if it is a painful one. When, however, the German women´s side managed to win the silver team medal in foil and the men the gold for the same weapon 24 hours later, all was right again with the world in Germany. The German male and female athletes could hardly contain their joy - jumping, laughing, waving and crying. And yet it was not merely rejoicing, but must also have contained a good measure of relief, the kind of relief anyone would feel after having pulled himself out of a deep valley of despair. Perhaps it was no such bad thing for some of the German fencing side to be reminded of how it feels to have to live with defeat. Not so much for the athletes themselves. They never really have any opportunity to forget that particular reality, as it forms so much a part of their everyday experience to be the one that failed to make it. But for those in charge of the athletes, it may have been a highly salutary if unwelcome lesson.

"gold medal factory", Annette Dobmeier and Zita Funkenhauser, had already been disposed of, so that to the obvious chagrin of the Germans, silver and gold went to Huifeng Wang and Tatiana Sadowskaja of China and the CIS respectively. Emil Beck, the German coach put it bluntly, "This is one of the biggest disappointments of my career".

Team Events

Beck's disappointment at the German failure to take any individual medal turned to triumph, however, when it came to the team events. The turning point for Germany came when the 23 year-old young mother, Anja Fichtel-Mauritz, twice victor at Seoul, led the women's foil team to win the silver medal. And this only 53 days after the birth of her son, Laurin. "I was immensely spurred on by being able to show up those who hadn't wanted to believe in me," she said, and yet she was a little disappointed not to win over the Italians, who took the gold. "We were so close," she said. There- after, matters steadliy improved for Germany in the team events. In the épée, they at first found it difficult to get the measure of their Hungarian opponents in the final. At 2:2, the Hungarians were left hoping. But those hopes were dashed by a concerted attack from a sometime Soviet member of the German team, Reznitchenko along with Schmidt, the German Olympic champion of 1988. Germany took the team gold medals in foil and épée. German inroads are steadily being made in the preserve of the traditional fencing nations.

RESULTS

Marin (ITA), Szabo (HUN) and Lamour (FRA) together on the podium with their medals from the sabre event. Szabo took the gold.

Together for the last time. The Unified Team which won the bronze in the sabre team event.

She came as world champion and left as Olympic champion. Italy's Giovanni Trillini (ITA) won convincingly in the foil.

A joint effort. The winners in the épée team contest (top). Consolation for Elmar Borrman (below) who just missed out on a medal in the individual contest.

Épée

Men's individual	01.08.1992
1. E. Srecki (FRA)	
2. P. Kolobkov (EUN)	
3. J.-M. Henry (FRA)	
4. K. Kaaberma (EST)	
5. E. Borrmann (GER)	
6. A. Mazzoni (ITA)	
7. M. Rivas Nieto (COL)	
8. I. Kovacs (HUN)	

Foil

Men's individual	31.07.1992
1. P. Omnes (FRA)	
2. S. Goloubitski (EUN)	
3. E. Gregory Gil (CUB)	
4. U. Wagner (GER)	
5. A. Borella (ITA)	
6. M. Sypniewski (POL)	
7. G. Betancourt Scull (CUB)	
8. J. Wendt (AUT)	

Sabre

Men's team	07.08.1992
1. EUN	Kirikenko · Tschirschov · Pogosov Gutzeit · Pozdniakov
2. HUN	Szabo · Köves · Nebald Abay · Bujdoso
3. FRA	Lamour · Daurelle · Ducheix Granger-Veyron · Guichot
4. ROM	
5. GER	
6. POL	

Foil

Women's individual	30.07.1992
1. G. Trillini (ITA)	
2. H. Wang (CHN)	
3. T. Sadovskaia (EUN)	
4. L. Modaine (FRA)	
5. M. Zalaffi (ITA)	
6. R. Z. Szabo (HUN)	
7. S. C. Bau (GER)	
8. F. J. McIntosh (GBR)	

Foil

Men's team	05.08.1992
1. GER	Weißenborn · Wagner · Weidner Koch · Schreck
2. CUB	Gregory · Betancourt · O. Garcia Diaz · H. Garcia
3. POL	Sypniewski · Kielpikowski Krzesinski · Sieß · Sobczak
4. HUN	
5. EUN	
6. ITA	

Sabre

Men's individual	02.08.1992
1. B. Szabo (HUN)	
2. M. Marin (ITA)	
3. J.-F. Lamour (FRA)	
4. G. Scalzo (ITA)	
5. A. Garcia Hernandez (ESP)	
6. F. Meglio (ITA)	
7. R. T. Koscielniakowski (POL)	
8. J. Nolte (GER)	

Épée

Men's team	07.08.1992
1. GER	Schmitt · Felisiak · Borrmann Reznitschenko · Proske
2. HUN	Kovacs · Kulcsar · Hegedius Koczonay · Totola
3. GUS	Chuwalov · Kokobov · Kostarev Kratchuk · Zakharevitch
4. FRA	
5. ITA	
6. ESP	

Foil

Women's team	04.08.1992
1. ITA	Trillini · Zalaffi · Bortolozzi Bianchedi · Vaccaroni
2. GER	Bau · Funkenhauser · Dobmeier Fichtel-Mauritz · Weber-Koszto
3. ROM	Szabo · Grigorescu · Tufan Badea · Dumitrescu
4. EUN	
5. FRA	
6. CHN	

Simon's double bronze

Simon Terry, an 18-year-old unemployed builder gave British archery a big boost by winning two bronze medals, one in the 70 metres individual event and the second in the men's 70-metre team event, along with Steven Hallard and Richard Priestman. The second medal was, in fact, a repeat of the team's performance in Seoul. For Terry, previously ranked 20th in Britain, it was an amazing achievement. To be amongst the medal winners was beyond his wildest fantasies. The Lincolnshire boy remarked: "It's not too bad winning too bronze medals in two days, But I don't want to make a habit of it. I'd rather win two golds." He had had plenty of time to devote to his sport and could claim to be one of the few people to have benefited from the recession. Despite the rich British archery heritage of Agincourt and Henry V's foot soldiers, it is 84 years since Britain won an archery medal.

Although medals for shooting are among the first to be awarded, sadly none of them were for the British team. British shooting enthusiasts will have to wait another four years for medals. Over the years, Britain has had an enviable record in the sport, having amassed a total of 46 medals, but now that Malcolm Cooper and Allister Allan have retired from the scene, British hopes have faded. Dominance in this discipline has been ceded to the Rus-

sians and the far eastern countries. Only just wide of the mark is still wide. Silvia Sperber, from Penzing in Bavaria, failed by one point to get into the final of the best eight in the women's air rifle competition. The winner was the 18 year-old Kab-Soon Yeo of South Korea who thus gained her country's first gold medal of this year's Games. "I just felt like sinking through the floor", admitted Germany's star of Seoul, after she had come only twentieth in her favourite event, the three-positions rifle competition.

Towards the end, his hand was shaking like a leaf. But with his last shot in the free pistol, Konstantin Lukashik of the Unified Team became at the tender age of 16,

From gold to silver: South Korea's Soo Nyung Kim had to be satisfied with second place. Four year's earlier in Seoul, she won the gold.

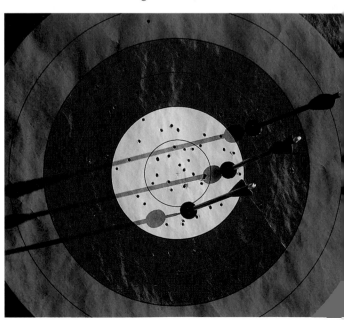

The woman with the golden gun

the youngest-ever winner in Olympic shooting history. His team-mate and twice world champion, Marina Logvinenko, on the other hand, clinically hit the target in the sport pistol final. The 30 year-old was the undisputed queen of a team, which dominated the whole competition, winning a total of five gold medals.

"I'm knackered", admitted Johann Riederer from Unterföhring afterwards. The reason for his exhaustion dangled around his neck. Despite an injury to his right eye, sustained in his youth from an explosives experiment that went terribly wrong, the 34-year-old postal worker from Bavaria was in the silver-medal position until just before the end. His last shot was good, but not quite good enough. Because of the air rifle competition's peculiar arithmetic, the twice-world champion once again had to be satisfied with a bronze medal, repeating his performance at Seoul.

Shan means mountain in Chinese. But it was more an earthquake which Zhang Shan caused to upset male pride in the women's target skeet final. The Chinese woman won the final and became the first woman to outscore the men.

Thanks to his yoga breathing exercises before that rapid-fire pistol competition, Ralf Schumann from the German town of Dudweiler was able to keep a cool head in the furnace of Mollet del Valles. Even in the year before Barcelona, no-one was able to pull the trigger five times in four seconds with the dexterity of this native of Saxony.

Above: Ralf Schumann,
the man with the rapid-fire pistol
and the golden shot.
Four years' earlier in Seoul,
he won the silver.

Far left: Shadowing with the free pistol.
Left: Petr Hrdlicka (TCH) hit the most clay-pigeons in the trap contest.

Above: Michael Jakosits from Homburg in Germany hit the running target for gold, Frenchman Franck Badiou (left) won the silver medal.

Eye and ear protection was not enough for Romanian, Sorin Babii (left). He only managed third place.

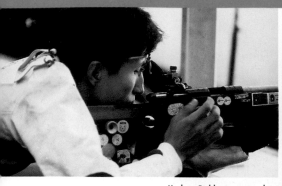

Herbert Bichler just missed out on the gold. In the end, Korean Eun-Chul Lee took the top prize.

Olympic champion in the rapid fire pistol. Wyatt Earp would have had no chance against Ralf Schumann (above).

Hans Riederer (above) repeated his Seoul success in the air rifle section.

Shang Zhang (CHI) wrote Olympic history: she was the first woman to score higher than a man in the skeet.

Running target

Men	01.08.1992
1. M. Jakosits (GER)	673
2. A. Asrabaev (EUN)	672
3. L. Racansky (TCH)	670
4. A. Vasiliev (EUN)	667
5. J. Sike (HUN)	667
6. J. Zimmermann (GER)	667

Air pistol

Men	28.07.1992
1. Y. Wang (CHN)	684.8
2. S. Pyjianov (EUN)	684.1
3. S. Babii (ROM)	684.1
4. H. Xu (CHN)	681.5
5. S. Paasonen (FIN)	680.1
6. J. Pietrzak (POL)	680.1
7. T. Kiryakov (BUL)	679.7
8. R. di Donna (ITA)	678.5

Air rifle

Men	27.07.1992
1. I. Fedkine (EUN)	695.3
2. F. Badiou (FRA)	691.9
3. J. Riederer (GER)	691.7
4. J. P. Amat (FRA)	691.6
5. G. Maksimovic (IOP)	690.5
6. T. Farnik (AUT)	690.2
7. R. J. Foth (USA)	689.4
8. Keun-Bae Chae (KOR)	687.8

Rifle 3 positions

Men	31.07.1992
1. G. Petikiane (EUN)	1267.4
2. R. Foth (USA)	1266.6
3. R. Koba (JPN)	1265.9
4. J. Hirvi (FIN)	1264.8
5. H. Stenvaag (NOR)	1264.6
6. R. Debevec (SLO)	1262.6

Free pistol

Men	26.07.1992
1. K. Loukachik (EUN)	658
2. Y. Wang (CHN)	657
3. R. Skanaker (SWE)	657
4. D. Young (USA)	655
5. S. Babii (ROM)	653
6. I. Agh (HUN)	652

Rapid fire pistol

Men	30.07.1992
1. R. Schumann (GER)	885
2. A. Kuzmins (LAT)	882
3. V. Vokhmianine (EUN)	882
4. D. Kucharczyk (POL)	880
5. J. T. McNally (USA)	781
6. M. Ignatiouk (EUN)	779

Rifle prone

Men	29.07.1992
1. Eun-Chul Lee (KOR)	702.5
2. H. Stenvaag (NOR)	701.4
3. S. Pletikosic (IOP)	701.1
4. H. Bichler (GER)	701.1
5. M. Bury (FRA)	700.0
6. J. P. Hirvi (FIN)	699.5

Archery

Men's individual	03.08.1992
1. S. Flute (FRA)	542
1. Jae-Hun Chung (KOR)	542
3. S. Terry (GBR)	528
4. B. Grov (NOR)	
5. J. Barrs (USA)	
6. H. Setijawan (INA)	
7. W. Chikarev (EUN)	
8. J. Lipponen (FIN)	

Archery

Men's team	04.08.1992
1. ESP	
Hodalgo · Vazquez Menendez	
2. FIN	
Falck · Lipponen Poikolainen	
3. GBR	
Priestman · Hallard Terry	
4. FRA	
5. KOR	
5. USA	
5. AUS	
5. EUN	

When the archers get their instructions to fire!

Bull's eye. One of the archers was pleased with this arrow, but how do you get it out?

French gold medallist in the archery, Sebastien Flûte. The new Robin Hood.

Simon Terry, British bronze medallist couldn't match his French opponent's skill.

Running target

Women	27.07.1992	
1. M. Logvenenko (EUN)		684
2. D. Li (CHN)		680
3. D. Munkhbayar (MGL)		679
4. M. Skoko (KRO)		677
5. N. Saloukvadze (EUN)		676
6. J. Sekaric (IOP)		676

Air pistol

Women	01.08.1992	
1. M. Logvinenko (EUN)		486.4
2. J. Sekaric (IOP)		486.4
3. M. Grousdeva (BUL)		481.6
4. L. Wang (CHN)		479.7
5. C. Kajd (SWE)		478.9
6. M. Fernandez (ESP)		478.5

Rifle 3 positions

Women	30.07.1992	
1. L. Meili (USA)		684.3
2. N. Matova (BUL)		682.7
3. M. Ksiazkiewicz (POL)		681.5
4. E. Forian (HUN)		679.5
5. S. Skoko (CRO)		678.7
6. V. Letcheva (BUL)		678.0

Archery

Women's team	04.08.1992
1. KOR Eun-Kyung Lee · Youn Cho Soo-Nyung Kim	
2. CHN Wang · Wang · Ma	
3. EUN Walejeva · Arjannikova Kwriwischwili	
4. FRA	
5. SWE	
6. USA	
7. PRK	
8. TUR	

Skeet

	28.07.1992
1. S. Zhang (CHN)	223
2. J. J. Giha Yarur (PER)	222
3. B. M. Rossetti (ITA)	222
4. I. Toman (ROM)	222
5. J. M. Colorado Gonzalez (ESP)	222
6. M. A. Dryke (USA)	221

Air rifle

Women	26.07.1992	
1. Kab-Soon Yeo (KOR)		498.2
2. V. Letcheva (BUL)		495.3
3. A. Binder (IOP)		495.1
4. D. Bilkova (CSFR)		494.9
5. V. Tcherkassova (EUN)		494.6
6. Eun-Ju Lee (KOR)		492.6

Trap

	02.08.1992
1. P. Hrdlicka (TCH)	219
2. K. Watanabe (JPN)	219
3. M. Venturini (ITA)	218
4. J. Damme (GER)	218
5. P. Kubec (TCH)	218
6. J. H. Waldron (USA)	217

Archery

Women's individual	02.08.1992
1. Youn-Jeong Cho (KOR)	552
2. Soo-Nyung Kim (KOR)	543
3. N. Valeeva (EUN)	526
4. X. Wang (CHN)	525

The man with the golden pedals

Cycling has featured in every modern Olympic Games, although today's programme bears little resemblance to Athens 1896. Then six races were contested by just 19 riders from five countries. The Greek hero of the first Games went by the name of Aristides Konstantinidis. He won the road race from Athens to Marathon and back on a cycle borrowed from a spectator, after he had wrecked his own by riding into a brick wall at full speed. It was some years before a standard programme emerged.

Britain's record has not been impressive in recent years, but there were high hopes that 1992 might see an improvement in the British team's medal tally. A lot of work had been going on behind the scenes.

First success

Just as the armchair critics were beginning to start complaining about the British team's lack of success in Barcelona, Chris Boardman, a cycle design consultant from Hoylake in the Wirral, won Britain's first gold medal of the Games. He caught the world champion, Jens Lehmann of Germany, with just under 250 metres to go in the final of the 4,000 metre individual pursuit. Not only was it a triumph for British cycling (it was 72 years since Britain had won an Olympic track medal in cycling), it was also a triumph for British design. The publicity accorded the revolutionary, aerodynamic cycle will bring Norwich-based Lotus Engineering a welcome boost to their export sales. Bicycle manufacturers around the world have been waging a technological battle for 10 years in an attempt to reduce times. Skin-tight suits, streamlined helmets, disc wheels and triathlon handlebars have only had limited success amongst the cycling fraternity.

Aerodynamic frame

The breakthrough came with the production of a carbon fibre monocoque frame, which is more aerodynamic than conventional frames. The bike weighs a mere 8 kg, with other parts made from titanium and aluminium. Additional features include a raised seat, so that the rider takes a prone position, thereby bringing the legs closer together and improving aerodynamics. A

The German quartet on the way to gold in the 100 kilometre team time trial (left).

100 kilometres under Barcelona's blazing sun. One of the French team which won the bronze recovering from his exertions.

Italian Fabio Casartelli (in front) brings home the gold in the road race beating Dutchman Eric Dekker.

single arm connects the frame to the front wheel, replacing the conventional twin forks.

The new machine aroused huge interest in Barcelona, but it will not be going on sale until after the Games. Doug Dailey, the British team captain, allayed fears that cycling was not just about to become dominated by technology. "Boardman is one of the physically strongest athletes I have ever met," he commented after the race. Even his arch rival and defeated World Champion, Jens Lehmann, said after the race: "It is his talent and not his bike which make him go so fast."

Anxious moments

Right: Chris Boardman, Britain's gold medal winner, on his dream machine.

There had been a few anxious moments before the race as the technical back-up men tinkered with their spanners. Boardman had to stand, wait and watch, before climbing aboard and watching for the start flag to drop. For the first few metres, he stood on the pedals. As soon as the bike was moving smoothly forward, he crouched low and flat, winning time from Lehmann almost immediately. After four laps, he had gained more than a second, and at halfway nearly three seconds. Barring accidents, the result was as certain. The digital

Top Dutch cyclist, Ingrid Haringa, sprints past Felicia Ballanger(13) from France to win the bronze.

clock recording the split times suddenly ceased to function, as if to save the German from any further embarrassment. By the 13th lap, Boardman sensed he could catch the German, which he duly did, punching the humid air as he swept in front. It was a blissful moment for Boardman, his wife and the British team. The last circuit of the wooden track set amid the scrubby hills above Barcelona turned into a lap

of honour for the 23 year-old Boardman. Nobody at the velodrome could recall such a decisive finish to an Olympic pursuit final. His face lit up with a smile, which did not fade as he wheeled round to embrace his wife at the trackside near the finishing line. His wife, Sally-Ann, had watched the record-breaking first heats on television at home, but decided that she had to be there and set off for Barcelona. "I wanted to see him do it, to win the gold medal," she told reporters. But she had to pay a ticket tout twice the face value for her ticket to get into the Val d'Hebron velodrome. It was 3,000 pesetas (£16)

well spent. But it was only a small price to pay, when set against the time and expense spent on training and working on the bike. He would, no doubt, have been reminded before mounting the podium that it was in a 2,000 metres tandem race, now discontinued, in the Antwerp Olympics of 1920 that Britain last won a cycling medal. The joy appeared to be replaced by a quieter awareness of the magnitude of what he had achieved.

New technology on trial

The individual pursuit is not an exciting event for the uninitiated. The riders set off on opposite sides of the track and try to catch each other up over 16 laps of 250m. It is all about beating the clock. The cameras and reporters were all drawn by the fascination of seeing whether the high expectations of the latest technology could meet the most demanding of tests. The German man's views on Boardman's ma-

Below: German team pursuit winners, led in by Jens Lehmann.
Below right: Not quite good enough. Dejected German, Jens Glücklich, came fourth in the 1 km time trial.

chine are probably unprintable. Lehmann must have felt that the Olympic title was his for the taking, when he won the World Championships in Stuttgart last year. Boardman's record up to Barcelona was the three bronze medals he had picked up from the last two Commonwealth Games. In the semi-final, the Briton had waltzed home after beating Mark Kingsland, an Australian, riding a bike that looked so old-fashioned by comparison, that it might as well have had a basket on the front handlebars and a baby seat over the rear mudguard. The German had to fight much harder in his semi-final against the New Zealander, Gary Anderson, and finished 3.831 seconds ahead, but Anderson performed well enough to win the bronze. The British officials, having guarded the three existing models of the super-bike from the threat of sabotage, could now relax.

Spanish success

Earlier in the week, the velodrome, about five miles outside central Barcelona, had become sacred land

for the local spectators, when José Manuel Moreno won the one kilometre time trial, the host country's first gold medal. Coming so soon after Miguel Indurain's victory in the Tour de France, the Spanish cyclists were well and truly kings. In return, Manuel Moreno dedicated his splendid victory to the Virgin Santa Ana, his family and the Spanish people.

The space-age machine was on its way home, when Boardman swapped it for something a little more conventional. He and teammates Paul Jennings, Bryan Steel and Glen Sword qualified as fifth fastest in the time trial to establish which eight teams would contest

the team 4,000m pursuit. Boardman admitted that sitting on a conventional bike was a bit of a shock to the system. Victory in the individual pursuit had left him 'stuffed'. "I just could not raise the pace," he told waiting reporters. In the final, Jens Lehmann took his revenge. The four Germans won the team gold medal, with Australia and Denmark taking the silver and bronze medals respectively. The British quartet came fifth.

The pleasure and the pain

The victory ceremony is a major life event for successful Olympic contestants - a full stadium, flags, bouquets, national anthems and the presentation of the precious metals. Years of personal sacrifice come to a climax in an occasion which will remain in the memory until the grave. The coveted medal will occupy pride of place on the mantelpiece alongside a photograph, the photograph, which captures for posterity that fleeting entry on to the world stage.

But if you were one of the cycling medal winners on the first morning of the Games, you would have felt distinctly let down. At one o'clock, all self-respecting Spaniards are taking shelter from the baking sun. It is siesta time. The stands were empty. Only a few of the real enthusiasts stayed on. After all, cycling fans are a very special breed of sportsperson. It must be a pleasure to sit under the relentless Mediterranean sun, rather than to push yourself and your machine up the hillsides or to pedal a dizzy path round the velodrome.

So it was for the four Germans who won the 100 kilometre road race. The champagne corks popped. The handful of fans who remained, cheered, as the four boys grinned and embraced each other. The cameras clicked, as memories were made. A few yards away, the Swedish team sat alongside their machines, their wheels and their discarded helmets. A closer look told the full story. They lay there in the shadowless stadium, heads buried in hands, their vests torn, their shoulders bleeding, their legs grazed and with tears in their eyes.

Australia's Kathy in gold-rush

Kathryn Watt of Australia launched a solo attack to win the women's road race title. Frenchwoman Jeannie Longo-Ciprelli, 8-times world champion on road and track, was clearly the favourite, but Watt, the Commonwealth champion, made her break on the final lap of the 16 kilometre circuit at Sant Sadurni d'Anoia to finish in 2hr 4min 42 seconds. In temperatures close to 40 degrees, she had become the first Australian to win a medal in the women's cycling events.

The 33 year-old Jeannie Longo, who had dominated the sport for most of the 80's, still managed a strong challenge a few kilometres from home, taking the lead from the Dutch woman, Monique Knol, the gold-medal winner from Seoul. In the end, neither could cope with the determination and strength of the Australian girl. Knol still finished ahead of the pack to win the bronze.

Watt was naturally delighted. "There's nothing to compare with this," she said. "I thought I'd take the chance of riding aggressively. No one in the pack seemed to do anything, so I went for it." Longo, with her reputation to defend, said afterwards that she was not disappointed. The other riders had not realised that Watt was ahead of them. "Nobody knew that Kathy was out in front." The French cyclist at least had something to take home from her two-wheeled tour of Catalonia and seemed satisfied with her medal. At Los Angeles in 1984, the chain came off her bike and in Seoul, she finished 21st after being troubled by injury.

Petra Rossner wins gold. The German woman cyclist on a victory circuit after winning the individual pursuit race.

The winning trio from the women's road race: Jeannie Longo-Ciprelli, Kathryn Watt and Monique Knol.

Chris Boardman from the Wirral. The first British gold medal winner in the track cycling events since 1920.

East meets West after the sprint. Estonia's Erika Salumae, the winner of the newly-independent Baltic republic's first medal, with the German girl, Annett Neumann.

Individual pursuit

Women	31.07.1992
1. P. Rossner (GER)	3:41.753
2. K. A. Watt (AUS)	3:43.438
3. R. Twigg (USA)	
4. H. Malmberg (DEN)	
5. J. Longo-Ciprelli (FRA)	
6. S. Samochvalova (EUN)	

Road race

Women	26.07.1992
1. K. Watt (AUS)	2:04.42
2. J. Longo-Ciprelli (FRA)	2:05.02
3. M. Knol (NED)	2:05.03
4. N. Kistchuk (EUN)	2:05.03
5. M. Valvik (NOR)	2:05.03
6. J. M. Golay (USA)	2:05.03

Sprint

Women	31.07.1992
1. E. Salumae (EST)	
2. A. Neumann (GER)	
3. I. Haringa (NED)	
4. F. Ballanger (FRA)	
5. G. Enukhina (EUN)	
6. T. Dubnicoff (CAN)	
7. N. Kuroki (JPN)	
8. Y. Wang (CHN)	

1km time trial

Men	27.07.1992
1. J. Moreno Periñan (ESP)	1:03.342
2. S. J. Kelly (AUS)	1:04.268
3. E. W. Hartwell (USA)	1:04.753
4. J. Glücklich (GER)	1:04.798
5. A. Capelli (ITA)	1.05.065
6. F. Lancien (FRA)	1:05.157
7. J. D. Andrews (NZL)	1:05.240
9. D.-J. van Hameren (NED)	1:05.524
14. A. A. Stirrat (GER)	1:06.522

Individual pursuit

Men	29.07.1992
1. C. M. Boardman (GBR)	4:27.357
2. J. Lehmann (GER)	4:30.054
3. G. Anderson (NZL)	
4. M. L. Kingsland (AUS)	
5. P. Ermenault (FRA)	
6. C. Mathy (BEL)	

Individual points race

Men	31.07.1992
1. G. Lombardi (ITA)	44
2. L. van Bon (NED)	43
3. C. Mathy (BEL)	41
4. G. McLeay (NZL)	30
5. L. Tesar (TCH)	30
6. E. Magnin (FRA)	24
7. G. Fulst (GER)	24
8. A. Aeschbach (SUI)	23

Road race

Men	02.08.1992
1. F. Casartelli (ITA)	4:35.21
2. E. Dekker (NED)	4:35.22
3. D. Ozols (LET)	4:35.24
4. E. Zabel (GER)	4:35.56
5. L. Aus (EST)	4:35.56
6. A. Sypykowski (POL)	4:35.56

Sprint

Men	31.07.1992
1. J. Fiedler (GER)	
2. G. Neiwand (AUS)	
3. R. Chiappa (ITA)	
4. C. Harnett (CAN)	
5. K. Carpenter (USA)	
6. J. Lovito (ARG)	

Team pursuit

Men	31.07.1992
1. GER Glöckner · Lehmann Steinweg · Fulst	4:08.791
2. AUS Aitken · McGlede O'Brien · O'Grady	4:10.218
3. DEN Frost · Madsen Petersen · Kynde	4:15.860
4. ITA	
5. GBR	
6. EUN	

100 km team time trial

Men	26.07.1992
1. GER Dittert · Meyer Peschel · Rich	2:01.39
2. ITA Anastasia · Colombo Contri · Peron	2:02.39
3. FRA Boussard · Faivre-Pierret Gaumont · Harel	2:05.25
4. EUN	2:05.34
5. ESP	2:06.11
6. POL	2:06.34

Top left: In the individual points race, the Dutch silver medallist, Leon van Bon, is wearing the orange top.

157

Matthew Ryan spells it out to his rivals

Australia were the unexpected winners of both the team and individual gold medals in the three day event competition. The British team, which had come to Barcelona with such high hopes of victory were left empty-handed. It was Matthew Ryan who sealed his country's triumph in both sections of the competition by jumping a cool round under extreme pressure. The Germans had to be content with the silver medal.

Eventing is the most arduous of the three disciplines. It incorporates a set dressage test on the first day, followed by speed and endurance tests across country on day two and on the final day, the show jumping. This last section reflects the military history of the sport, with horse and rider having to show that, despite their exertions of the previous two days, they have conserved enough energy to fight another day.

Glory days

In previous Olympic eventing contests, the British have maintained a good record. Richard Meade won the individual gold in Munich in 1972 and there have been three team golds, in 1956, 1968 and 1972. The hopes of the British team rested very largely on the head of Ian Stark. The 37-year-old Scot broke a sequence of individual silver and bronze medals at Punchestown Ireland last year, when he won the elusive gold as

the European champion. Having spent the earlier years of his working life in the Civil Service, in 1982, he left his desk to concentrate full-time on competitive riding. In his first Badminton in 1984, he finished third and sixth, earning a place in that year's Olympic silver medal team. Since then, he has won Badminton twice and has been a regular member of Britain's top teams.

Dutch show-jumper Piet Raymakers on his way to the team gold (left). It wasn't the German team's day. Ludger Beerbaum came off the worst. His horse, Classic Touch, suffered a broken bridle (below).

The course (below) in the show jumping did not get an enthusiastic reception from riders or horses.

Favourite Nick Skelton on Dollar Girl (above) fell at the water jump. Ludger Beerbaum (right) on Classic Touch maintained his composure.

Strong nerves and a strong horse on his way to victory in the individual show jumping contest.

Stark choice for Murphy Himself

Murphy Himself gets his pension book

But his challenge in Barcelona ended with the depressing sight of Murphy Himself failing the horse inspection. The venerable dappled grey was found to be suffering from an inflamed tendon after his cross-country round, which had secured second place for the British team when they were only eight points adrift of New Zealand. Stark was in fifth place and chasing an individual medal. Ironically, Stark had announced the previous night that Murphy Himself would be withdrawing from competitive eventing. He had not realised that the vet would be handing over the grey's pension book a little earlier than expected.

Matt Ryan takes the gold

But the fortunes of the New Zealander also came painfully down to earth. In the final stage of the event, Andrew Nicholson on Spinning Rhombus scattered poles around the arena, thereby incurring 45 penalties for nine mistakes. His team fell from second position to 16th. As a consequence of Spinning Rhombus' wild fling, the German, Herbert Blöcker, moved up to second place and received the individual silver medal on Feine Dame. Another New Zealander, Blyth Tait, whose individual hopes seemed to have gone, when his mount Messiah misbehaved in the dressage, made a dramatic move to take the bronze medal. He had started 69th after the dressage before progressing to eighth in the

The cross-country made heavy demands. The French rider, Boisson on Oscar de la Log (left) had difficulty keeping control!

It has never done before - winning four medals with same rider on the same horse. Nicole Uphoff and Rembrandt performed this amazing feat in the dressage.

cross-country and then jumped a clear round to finish third.

But the new champion, Matt Ryan on the 15-year old gelding Kibah Tic Toc, put to one side memories of a disastrous performance at Badminton earlier this year. His only error came at the last fence and it made no difference to the outcome. Ryan is a youthful-looking 28-year-old with a broad smile. He is a country boy from New South Wales and according to the Olympic handbook lists his occupation as 'farmhand'. His hobbies, he says, are cricket, golf and spelling. Despite his rural background, he seemed to be on good enough terms with his rivals in the British team. Almost the first with a kiss for Ryan after it had become clear that he had won, were the two British women.

Australia last won a gold medal in the three-day eventing in 1960 in Rome, when they also triumphed in both the team and individual competitions. Laurie Morgan was the hero on that occasion. Matthew Ryan could so easily have been left at home with his spelling primer.

NED v GER in the show jumping

Nicole Uphoff and Isabell Werth (right) are the two top German women in the dressage, but Isabell had to play second fiddle.

The showjumping produced some surprises, not least for one of the British hopes. Joint favourite, Nick Skelton was eliminated. after his highly-regarded Hanoverian Dollar Girl refused to jump a particularly hazardous water jump. It was the first time he had ever been known to stop. This came as a desperate blow after the horse had cleared thirteen of the fourteen fences with

spot on accuracy. The German team, winners in Seoul, will want to forget Barcelona. Ludger Beerbaum had to lead his horse, Classic Touch off the ring on foot after it broke its bridle in the second round. The American team, which had selected its team using computers only managed sixth place. The Netherlands won their first Olympic gold medal for show jumping with Jos Lansink showing marvellous composure. In the individual show jumping final, Ludger Beerbaum with Classic Touch made up for the disaster in the team event by winning the gold and pushing the Dutchman Piet Raymakers into second position.

Piaffes, pirouettes and passages

While others battle for seconds and millimetres, goals and baskets, in the dressage arena of the Polo Club, other qualities are required. Whose horse will dance the most beautiful piaffes, pirouettes and

passages? In the dressage square the aesthetes get their money's worth. The team competition lasted for two days. The highly-fancied Germans won, which was not that remarkable, but the extent to which they outclassed the opposition was spectacular. The United States won the bronze medal.

The team competition already foreshadowed the duel between Germany's two queens of dressage: 25-year-old Nicole Uphoff, who won in Seoul on Rembrandt. Rembrandt is a 15-year-old Westphalian, a horse like velvet, beautiful, noble but sometimes very headstrong. Her 23-year-old German rival, Isabell Werth, rides the self-confident and dynamic nine-year-old Hanoverian Gigolo.

Grand Prix

The Grand Prix Special, an exercise in which one obstacle follows another, decides the individual medal. Only riders and horses who are in perfect harmony can complete the course without errors. The scene is set for high drama. The best riders perform last, and last of all is Nicole Uphoff. Anky van Grunsven from the Netherlands is the first medal contender to ride. Her horse completes the movements light-footedly and obediently. It is clear that it has great potential. Next to ride is Balkenhol, a police sergeant. The striped Goldstern gives its best. When Balkenhol finishes, one thing seems certain – that was worth at least the bronze medal.

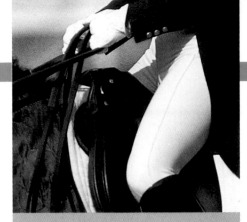

Highly-strung Rembrandt

The stadium goes very quiet. Rembrandt enters. Like so many stars he is highly-strung. The clicking of cameras, restless spectators, colourful flowers on the edge of the square, any of these can unnerve him. It would not be the first time that he has let his rider down. But Uphoff already noticed in the earlier rounds that Rembrandt likes this square. Everything that might disturb him is far away, no unusual noises frighten him. Rembrandt's daily routine takes account of his complex character. First a little light training, then an easy ride and a nibble of some grass on the green polo lawn. The exercise begins. Rembrandt is all there, wide awake yet still calm. It is a ride which the Swiss judge, Wolfgang Niggli, will later confess, sent a shiver down his spine. The square becomes a stage. Effortlessly, Rembrandt dances towards the gold. Everything looks so easy. No one can imagine the amount of work and effort that has gone into it. Later Uphoff says that, "Rembrandt performed the final movements all on his own, I could do nothing more." After the final salute, the crowd breaks into loud applause. The scoreboard shows 1626 points, 75 more than Isabell Werth. Nicole Uphoff and Rembrandt have won their fourth gold medal. After the victory ceremony, Uphoff pulls the other two medal winners on to the podium with her and embraces them. As a symbol of the whole world, as it were.

One man and his horse

On this occasion, the equestrian sports were held very close to the main events, just a few minutes away from the Olympic stadium. An atmospheric, if not especially large equestrian stadium was created out of the feudal surroundings of the Real Club de Polo. All but the dressage and the cross-country events were held here. From dawn to dusk on the large lawn, where the polo matches are normally held, the quadruped athletes were led, lunged and ridden. When not performing, the horses were accommodated in spacious, cool and carefully guarded stables. They enjoyed the round-the-clock attendance of a whole team of vets. Just like the people, some of the horses suffered considerably from the heat, which led the vets present to make an official request to the jury for greater consideration to be given to the horses. The medals were won by favourites, or by riders who have been part of the scene for some time. There were no opportunities here for Johnny-come-latelies. For success in equestrianism depends on the established relationship between horse and rider. That is something which distinguishes this sport from all other Olympic disciplines. For in those, an athlete has to rely only on his own strength and skill, or occasionally also on the technical excellence of his equipment. In equestrianism, however, winning is only possible with the active co-operation of a horse. Equestrianism is destined to continue as an Olympic sport, in spite of the huge cost of the facilities.

Pavel Skrzypaszek (left and below) did not actually win any disciplines, but showed a high overall consistency.

The horse is chosen for the rider, so that there is an element of chance in the equestrian event.

The Modern Pentathlon finds its origin in military lore. The story goes that a soldier has to deliver a message. He sets off by horse, dismounts for a swordfight, shoots his way out of further trouble, swims across a river and, finally, delivers his message after running across country to deliver his message. The riding now comes last. This section, which is something of a lottery, is always contentious. Unlike other equestrian sports competitors, in the Modern Pentathlon, the competitors do not ride their own horses, but draw lots for animals they have never seen before.

There have been some notorious incidents in this event. In 1972, a German competitor attacked his mount, when it refused to jump a fence. Then in Seoul, a Soviet star by the name of Boris Onishenko, tampered with the electronic equipment, so that his épée would register a hit, even if no hit was made. The British team have a history of performing well, winning the gold in 1976 in Montreal and the bronze in Seoul. However, this year, their performance was disappointing. Edouard Zenovka from the Unified Team was widely tipped to win the individual medal and had the highest score before the riding, but the unpredictable riding event pushed Zenovka down to third place. The gold medal winner was the Pole, Arkadiusz Skrzypaszek. Graham Brookhouse was the top-placed Briton, coming 8th, beating Richard Phelps, who came 13th. The team title was also won by the Poles with the British team in sixth place.

RESULTS

Michel Robert on Nonix (above) was a member of the successful French team.

Two victors. Piet Raymakers (above) and Hervé Godignon (top right).

Ludger Beerbaum went from being an unlucky loser in the team show jumping to winner in the individual contest.

An unusual angle on the horse in the equestrian event. The main thing is getting over the fence.

Show jumping

Team	09.02.1992
1. NED Raymakers · Romp Tops · Lansink	12.00
2. AUT Boor · Münzner Simon · Frühmann	16.75
3. FRA Godignon · Bourdy Robert · Navet	24.75
4. ESP	25.50
5. USA	28.00
5. SUI	28.00

Dressage

Individual	09.02.1992
1. N. Uphoff (GER)	1626
2. I. Werth (GER)	1551
3. K. Balkenhol (GER)	1515
4. A. v. Grunsven (NED)	1447
5. K. Kyrklund (FIN)	1428
6. C. Lavell (USA)	1408

Show jumping

Individual	09.02.1992
1. L. Beerbaum (GER)	0.00
2. P. Raymakers (NED)	0.25
3. N. Dello Joio (USA)	4.75
4. H. Godignon (FRA)	6.25
5. J. Tops (NOR)	8.25
6. M. Gretzer (SWE)	10.25
7. L. Philippaerts (BEL)	12.25
8. M. Jensen (DEN)	12.75

Dressage

Team	09.02.1992
1. GER Uphoff · Theodorescu Werth · Balkenhol	5224
2. NED Bartels · van Grunsven Sanders · Bontje	4742
3. USA Lavell · Bredahl Poulin · Dover	4643
4. SWE	4537
5. DEN	4533
6. SUI	4524

Three day event

Individual	30.07.1992
1. M. Ryan (AUS)	70.00
2. H. Blöcker (GER)	81.30
3. B. Tait (NZL)	87.60
4. V. Latta (NZL)	87.80
5. A. Hoy (AUS)	89.40
6. K. Dixon (GBR)	92.40
7. L. Alvarez (ESP)	102.20
8. K. Donckers (NZL)	104.40
9. M. Thomson (GBR)	105.40
10. J. Desmedt (BEL)	108.40

Three day event

Team	30.07.1992
1. AUS Green · Rolton · Hoy Ryan	288.60
2. NZL Nicholson · Latta · Tait Todd	290.80
3. GER Baumann · Mysegaes Ehrenbrink · Blöcker	300.30
4. BEL	333.05
5. ESP	388.80
6. GBR	406.60

Modern pentathlon

Team	09.02.1992
1. POL Czycowicz · Skrzypaszek Gozdziak	16018
2. EUN Starostine · Svatkovski Zenovka	15924
3. ITA Tiberta · Massullo Bomprezzi	15760
4. USA	15649
5. HUN	15571
6. GBR	15571

Modern pentathlon

Individual	29.07.1992
1. A. Skrzypaszek (POL)	5559
2. A. Mizser (HUN)	5446
3. E. Zenovka (EUN)	5361
4. A. Starostine (EUN)	5347
5. R. Bomprezzi (ITA)	5326
6. H. Norebrink (SWE)	5321

The professionals didn't impress

Racket abuse. In the final, Jennifer Capriati, the American teenager got the better of Wimbledon champion Steffi Graf.

No hard feelings. Steffi was in a hurry in the semi-finals-kisses and a bronze medal for Mary-Joe Fernandez.

Tennis regained its Olympic status at the Seoul games in 1988. It had parted company from the Olympic movement at the Paris Games in 1924, when the tennis federations felt that their players were not receiving·the treatment they deserved. At the time, the women's changing rooms consisted of one wooden shed, which had to be locked during matches because there was no one to look after security, and the courts themselves were situated on a patch of wasteland. It was also one of the first sports to realise its true potential in terms of professional status and marketing. The amount of money that tennis generates in prizes is matched in professional sport only by that of golf and

Formula One racing. Player endorsements of products, from sporting goods to underwear, can net millions of pounds. Tournaments 'earn' revenue by selling the television rights and merchandise for a vast profit.

Professional rule

By the mid-1980's, tennis had evolved into the world's best example of the way in which a sport could be run to provide maximum profit at minimum cost. In almost every conceivable way, tennis has moved as far away from the amateur ethos of Olympic sport as it is possible to get. However, by 1988 the Olympic movement was in a position not only to allow tennis to return to the Olympic area, but to take it in with open arms. This change in status was forced on the IOC through economic necessity. Unfortunately, but all too foreseeably, the Games overall had to become profitable in order to survive. The Montreal Olympics of 1976 had been a disaster. The city's tax-payers are still footing the bill for the enormous debts that the city incurred. They were the last Olympiad to be financed solely by local government. In 1980, the Moscow Olympics were state-funded and the financial costs were never really an issue.

Excitement ahead

At Barcelona, however, tennis' contribution to the Games was by no

means merely financial. Vall d'Hebron and the tournaments were expected to be as exciting as any Grand Slam, particularly in the men's events where the field was short of only one leading player. André Agassi, who won Wimbledon, was not ranked high enough, at the time of selection to merit automatic inclusion in the American team.

The missing women

In the women's tournament, the field was not quite at full strength. Owing to a power struggle between the International Tennis Federation and some of the top women players, some of the famous names were absent. Monica Seles, Gabriela Sabatini and Martina Navratilova failed to make themselves available for the Federation Cup held in Britain last year. This was regarded by the ITF as the qualifying criterion for the women, and those who failed to attend were deemed ineligible for the Olym-

pics. However, there was still a strong presence in spite of these absences.

Gold for Capriati

In the Barcelona Olympics, the women's singles event was won by the 16-year-old American, Jennifer Capriati, who thereby became the youngest-ever tennis gold medallist. Despite claims that no title retains its full value when Seles, Sabatini and Navratilova are absent, (Seles is particularly strong on a clay court), it is generally assumed that this, the biggest win so far in the young American's short professional career, could well be the springboard she needs to start making serious challenges for Grand Slam titles. Capriati has been on the professional circuit for well over a year now, and having had a lot of help from, among many others, Chris Evert, it has been a period of learning rather than winning. But this has to be seen in perspective. Any other young professional would regard the Wimbledon semi-final as the height of ambition and yet this year Capriati has already achieved that ambition.

This Olympic final was a hard and exciting match. Capriati showed the spirit and determination to carry on fighting that has come with the many months she has spent following the tennis circus around the world. In the first set, Capriati allowed Graf to save nine break points in the fifth game, letting what appeared to be her best chance of victory slip by, which was empha-

sised when she let Graf break her serve in the eighth game with a double fault. She made a remarkable comeback, however, in the second set, playing strongly and steadily on the baseline and looking the better server. In the fifth game of the second set, Capriati finally broke the German's serve,

winning the game and going on to win the set. The third set was the hardest of the match. The confidence which in years before had seen Graf through many tight situations seemed to be lacking. With the score at 4-4, she netted two returns of her own serve and then doublefaulted. As the tension mounted in the stadium, she clawed back to deuce, but Capriati refused to give in and took the game, gaining the decisive break. The final score was 3-6, 6-3, 6-4. It was the first ever Olympic singles match that Steffi Graf had lost, having won the Los Angeles demonstration tournament

Advantage men. Coping with the heat is easier for the men. They can change their tops and throw water over themselves, but what do the women do?

in 1984, and winning the gold medal in Seoul. Graf considers that victory to have been the turning point in her career. Many will feel that Capriati could be on her way to emulating Miss Graf's achievements.

Local girl Arantxa's hopes dashed

Barcelona-born Arantxa Sanchez Vicario had high hopes of achieving success in front of her home fans. Many other Spanish contestants had been boosted by the support of the locals and the overall Spanish medals total bore little resemblance to that of Seoul. She reached the semi-finals and faced the eventual winner, Jennifer Capriati. The match was interrupted by the arrival of the Spanish King and Queen. "I thought they could have waited til the game ended," said Capriati. But their presence did little to help. She had begun horribly and finished worse. Capriati won 6-3, 3-6, 6-1.

She progressed further in the doubles, but the final was won by

the American pairing of Gigi Fernandez and Mary Joe Fernandez, who beat the top-seeded Barcelona girl and her partner Conchita Martinez. Again, the pair were not lacking for support, but were unable to live up to expectations, going down by 7-5, 2-6, 6-2.

Outsiders in the final

The men's tournament did not go as planned. In controversial circumstances, surrounding allegations that the top players cared little for the Olympic final, Becker, Stich, Sampras and Courier all went without attaining medal positions. The final was played out between two relative unknowns, Marc Rosset, a 21-year-old Swiss and a Spanish player, Jordi Arrese. Although both players linger some way down the rankings, they were evenly matched and appeared to realise that

Unity in diversity

Who can honestly complain at the fact that the two tennis players, Michael Stich and Boris Becker, do not share the same interests off the court? It is surely of no possible relevance if one man allows his feelings free reign or the other is unfailingly guided by reason – so what? The two Wimbledon champions soon lost their singles matches in the deep sands of the recreation grounds of the Vall d'Hebron against opponents whose strength lie on this type of surfaceThere must have come a point when they decided to put up serious opposition together – that point is unlikely to have been reached over coffee or lunch. Rather, it may have come in the course of a men's doubles match. For it was here that they beat the two Spaniards on the very sand surface that the locals had intended for the home players' benefit. Or the crucial point may have been reached when Becker took the initiative and propped up Stich. Or perhaps it was later still, during the encounter with the two Argentinians, where Stich reigned supreme and himself spurred Becker on. Both matches ran to five long sets, and nothing brings two people together like waging a bitter battle side by side. This was apparent even to outsiders, as the two men discussed tactics or, congratulated each other. All of a sudden they were in pursuit of a common goal and nothing else mattered. So perhaps there is something after all in what we fondly like to call the Olympic ideal.

Two Wimbledon champions, Michael Stich and Boris Becker won the men's doubles.

Two highly-motivated professionals used to playing for big money, joined forces to win a small gold-plated disc.

Marc Rosset eclipses Wimbledon stars

this might well be their only chance of appearing in a major final. The five-set match that they produced was highly exciting and lasted for over five hours. Rosset went into a two-set lead and the match seemed to be out of the reach of the young Spaniard. However, Arrese had a point to prove, after taking some criticism in the Spanish press for being selected ahead of another player who was more ranked highly. Perhaps this provided the spur for Arrese in fighting back to take the next two sets and level the match. In the final set, however, it was the Swiss player who dealt with the pressure best, taking the match with a final score of 7-6, 6-4, 3-6, 4-6, 8-6.

In the men's doubles, two of the big names who had failed to achieve what was expected of them in the singles raised their game to take the gold. Boris Becker and Michael Stich overcame their public animosity to beat the South African pairing of Wayne Ferreira and Piet Norval 7-6, 4-6, 7-6, 6-3.

British hopes dashed

Unfortunately for British followers of tennis, Barcelona did not offer even a glimmer of hope that our prospects are improving. The British presence here was lamentable. Of the five matches played, only one player made the second round and that was because a kind draw allowed Samantha Smith to beat Sara Gomer by 2-6, 6-3, 6-1. Apart from that match, in total, Britain won a mere three sets and lost 13, won 50 games and lost 92.

A picture is worth a thousand words. Becker and Stich celebrate after winning their final with the South African pair, Wayne Ferreira and Piet Norval (left).

Chinese women sweep the board

The Chinese proved yet again that they have women's table tennis completely sewn up. But strangely enough, the biggest threat to Chinese supremacy came from their own countrymen and women, those who had emigrated. China has been in the forefront of women's table tennis for more than four decades, though it has only been recognised as an Olympic sport since 1977 and was only staged for the first time at Seoul in 1988. Yet during that time, hundreds of coaches and players have found their way to the West.

In view of this fact, and the fact that the men's event is dominated by Europeans, China decided to use its right to veto the appearance of any ex-Chinese who had been living in the west for less than three years. This eliminated Chen Xinhua, a former world cup winner who is now the English national champion and Geng Lijuan, former Chinese champion, who is now the leading Canadian player. However, Wang Xiaoming, representing France now, because she is married to a Parisian journalist, was considered a force to be reckoned with, and she had left the People's Republic before the veto rule applied.

What's more, in last year's World Championships the women's world team title went to the united Korean team. However, China's Deng Yaping won the women's singles, beating the South Korean Hui Li-Bun and the women's doubles with victory going to Chen Zhie and Gao Jun. The mixed doubles were again won by the Chinese pair, Liu Wei and Wang Tao. There are no team table-tennis events or mixed doubles in the Olympic Games.

Petite gold medallist

In the end, China found that in the women's events, it had absolutely nothing to fear from foreign challenges. Deng Yaping and Qiao Hong won the women's double for China, and the women's singles final was an all-Chinese affair with Deng Yaping, 19-years-old and only 1.55 tall, challenging her com-

Frenchman Gatien (left) and Swede Jan-Ove Waldner prevented the Asians from sweeping the board in Barcelona. The Swedish royal family were among the spectators for the final.

Waldner lets go (below). The 'Mr Nice Guy' of Swedish table-tennis crowns his career with gold in the men's singles.

Swedish star resists Chinese challenge

patriot and erstwhile doubles partner. The fiercely aggressive Deng nearly lost points for her habit of doing a little dance before serving, which has earned her a yellow card in previous matches.

Deng's victory was decisive, making this her second Olympic gold and China's third in table tennis in these Olympics, since the Chinese had already won the men's doubles. Deng, the world champion and top seed, was able to receive her gold medal personally from Juan Antonio Samaranch, President of the International Olympic Commitee.

Deng uses the western tennis-style grip on the bat, instead of the traditional Chinese 'penholder-style' grip. Deng's father, who trained her, felt it would help to her combat her lack of inches. The British hopes for the doubles, Lisa Lomas and Andrea Holt, didn't have a chance, although Lomas was a silver medallist in the European championships. It is rumoured that the Chinese consider they have table tennis so firmly under control that the authorities decide which particular player is to be allowed to win the gold. Any other Chinese player who does better than the 'favourite' is supposedly penalised. This claim has been made by, among others, He Zhili, who won the 1987 world title despite instructions. She believes this is the reason why she was rejected for the Seoul Olympics team.

Snaky Swedish serve

In the men's single title, however, the Chinese have lost their leading

position. The men's event was won by Jan-Ove Waldner of Sweden, who originally broke the Chinese stranglehold in 1989, when he won the men's world championships. He beat the favourite, Frenchman Jean-Philippe Gatien, whom the experts had noticed has been playing particularly well this season. Gatien claimed to be put off by Waldner's snaky serve. Gatien in turn beat Ma Wenge, the Chinese challenger into third place. Waldner claimed this was the best performance of his career. It was Sweden's first gold medal in the games. "I think the Olympic title has already become as important as the world title and may become more important", explained Waldner.

The British male competitors included Carl Prean, the favourite who is ranked 23rd in the world and 2nd in Britain. Prean, aged 24, from the Isle of Wight, plays professionally for Steinhagen in the German Bundesliga, and is the son of John Prean who was the British table tennis team manager at the 1988 Seoul Olympics. Matthew Syed, an Oxford University undergraduate, was another British player tipped to do well. This was supposedly the best British men's team for 30 years, but they were completely outclassed, despite having invented the game. A familiar story! It is supposed to have been started by Cambridge University students, but they used textbooks instead of bats and called the game Gossima.

The much-fancied Swedish pair were knocked out in the early rounds of the men's doubles. The way was left open for Lu Lin and Wang Tao (below).

Tears instead of gold. Jörg Rosskopf and Stefan Fetzner (above) suffered at the hands of the Chinese pair, Lu Lin and Wang Tao.

Baseball is a simple game — throw, catch and run, but the Europeans still have a long way to go.

In the all-American game, the USA had to play second fiddle to their Cuban neighbours. Many of the league stars had to stay at home.

Italy's match against the USA was a good advert for this Olympic event.

Home run for the Cubans

Most people seemed to think that the ideological differences, which had always marred most of the post-war Olympic games had ended in Barcelona. But with the introduction of baseball on to the Olympic calendar, one political battle still remains to be fought. Cuba, world champions and Pan-American champions, would probably also have been Olympic champions had it not been for the political boycotts of '84 and '88. Like it or not, the Cuba - USA confrontation was likely to become a private feud. The pressure on the USA team, gold medal winners in Seoul, was intense. The American team, the cream of the college élite, were waiting for the end of the Games to put their signatures to some of the most lucrative sporting contracts in the world. Cuba's best players, Antonio Pacheco and Omar Ajete, could have made fortunes in the American league. In the semi-finals, the USA were still outclassed by the Cubans losing 6-1. Such is the fanatical interest in baseball, that the Cuban government had taken precautions to ensure that none of the many power cuts which affect the nation, occurred during the Olympic television coverage. During July, special measures were taken to conserve energy supplies, not for the sake of Cuban industry, but for the finals and semi-finals of the Olympic baseball competition. After the resounding victory against the Americans, defeating the Taiwanese in the final proved to be even less demanding for the Cuban squad. Cuba won 11-1.

The Cubans (above and extreme right), now the new Olympic champions, celebrate after defeating the 'class enemy' in the semi-final.

Spanish team fells Poles for gold

The football tournament is in many ways the biggest enigma of the entire Olympics. Football is probably the most popular sport in the world, and the World Cup Finals, which also take place every four years, is the only sporting event that can match or better the Olympic Games for world-wide public interest. Yet the Olympic football tournament has never gained the prestige one might imagine. For some reason, the sport does not seem to generate a great deal of excitement in such close proximity to so many other sports.

A mixed response to Olympic football

Football is a highly popular sport in Europe, and Spain in particular has an enormous love for the game, yet in this Olympics, the football tournament has had a particularly low profile. Matches played in the city of Barcelona were held at the Camp Nou stadium, which is the home to Barcelona Football Club, the current European Champions and the one of the biggest and most famous football clubs in the world. The city of Barcelona has a reputation for a love of football equalled only in Spain by the city of Madrid, but the highest attendance figure for any of the group matches was 28,000, which not surprisingly, was a match involving Spain. Many of the other matches, which have been placed around Spain in places such as Valencia and Zaragoza have attracted far smaller crowds. This has been a source of embarrassment to the tournament organisers, and for football in general. It is particularly damaging to the individuals charged with the planning, promotion

The Spanish team won the top prize in the football competition. They had the luxury of playing in front of their own exuberant supporters.

Goal!
....but hardly anyone saw it. Almost all of the games were played in front of empty stands.

and organisation of the next World Cup which will be held in the U.S.A. in 1994. The popularity of soccer tends to fall and rise in the United States in a fairly dramatic way. When the 1984 Olympics were held in Los Angeles, the game Americans always refer to as soccer to distinguish it from American football had the highest attendance figures of any sport within the games, including the athletics. It was not unusual for matches to have close to, or in excess of 100,000 spectators. This came after a slump in the popularity of football as a spectator sport in the States following the original boom in the mid-seventies. Since then, the USA's attitude to non-American football has been less and less favourable, probably because the World Cups in Mexico 1986 and Italy 1990 and the Olympic competition in Seoul in 1988 failed to excite any particular interest. The Americans had hoped that this tournament would provide

the kind of excitement needed to make the next World Cup a success.

The competition for the under-23's

The history of football in the Olympics is one of regular change since the entry of professional players into the Games. The tournament is now only open to players under the age 23, who have not played in any World Cup final matches. Players can, however, have played professionally, and many countries use their national under–21 team (which is allowed to have two 'over age' players in it) in the competition. The previous complicated rules about age and amateur status have been abolished. Despite this, there has been no British interest in the competition for many years. The strong aversion to the formation of a Great Britain team comes from the National Associations of the Home Countries and stems from a fear that

That wasn't a foul. Honest!
The referee was not
influenced by the Italian's
remonstrations.

Football - Olympic style

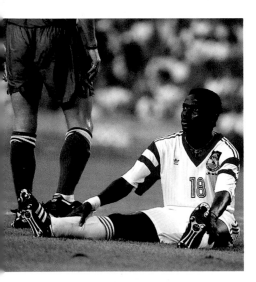

Australia's footballers suffered at the hands of the Ghanaian side. The Spanish heat sapped the player's strength.

The atmosphere returned when the Spanish team played. They beat Poland 3-2 in the final.

its presence would heighten pressure on FIFA to stop England, Scotland, Northern Ireland and Wales entering competitions in their own right, and thereby losing their individual votes on football's governing body.

African challenge

The tournament started on a controversial note. The pre-tournament favourites, Italy, had two men sent off, whilst on the very first weekend of the competition, Spain, the host country, and Colombia were disqualified from the fair play award after three players were sent off and nine others booked.

From the eight teams that qualified from the various groups, Spain, Italy, Poland, Qatar, Ghana, Paraguay, Sweden and Australia, the final four emerged as Ghana playing Australia for the bronze and Poland playing Spain for the gold and silver. In a close match, the Ghanaians edged out Australia 1-0 for the bronze. In an extremely exciting and close final, Spain initially fell behind to a goal from Poland's Kowalczyk in the 35th minute, but drew level and then edged into the lead through goals from Guardiola and Narvaez, midway through the second half. The possibility of extra time seemed likely to become a reality until a chip over the goalkeeper from Albert Ferrer in the very last minute of the game brought Spain their first ever gold medal in the football tournament. In contrast to the opening rounds, the final, played at the Camp Nou Stadium, drew an audience of 95,000.

Football in Spain is not just another sport. It's a way of life. That is particularly true in Barcelona, Spain's second city and home of FC Barcelona based at the Camp Nou stadium - the second biggest stadium in the world. The stadium must be seen to be believed. The huge stands tower above the pitch on which Barcelona play their league games. It ought not to be thought that Barcelona's home matches are in any way different to the other matches that take place on a Saturday afternoon elsewhere in Europe. But there is one difference: even when FC Barcelona are playing their regular home fixtures, there are likely to be at least 80,000 spectators all seated in this magnificent stadium and they express their displeasure by keeping their thoughts and feelings to themselves. When those same spectators sat and watched the final of this Olympic event, it was a different matter. The stands were not as full as they would have been, had FC Barcelona been at home to Real Madrid. Spain were playing Poland and the spectators had just been witnessing a whole host of other sports. They cheered, they suffered and they laughed, and when the home side scored the decisive goal only minutes before the final whistle, it sounded the same as in any other of the sports halls and stadia. The señores who were sitting in their usual places will have been surprised by what they heard. They may well have got the impression that the game of football would be a lot better off without the millionaire professionals who were absent this time.

Sixsmith hits two for third place

For the third time, the Australian men's hockey team reached the final, but this time they took the silver.

The German men's hockey team celebrating after their gold medal win. It had taken 20 years to win back the Olympic title.

The British women's hockey team upstaged the men by taking a surprise bronze medal. They did it by beating the South Koreans 4-3 after extra time. Janet Sixsmith's two goals brought victory to a British team that had fallen a goal behind on two occasions. It was a courageous performance, if at times a little careless. The entertaining game was characterised by the brilliance of Jane Sixsmith and the determination of Wendy Fraser. The aggression and poor finishing was evident from early on and the Koreans went one goal ahead in the fourth minute. South Korea, who had been beaten in the semi-final by Spain, played with flair and determination in the first half. But Sixsmith combined with Sandie Lister to slam the ball past the Korean keeper only minutes after the Korean goal. It was an unbelievable goal and desperately needed at that early stage of the game. The game continued to see-saw and extra-time loomed, something which the British team had feared given the temperature in the high eighties. Britain's coach, Dennis Hay said with a broad Scottish smile: "It was a great team performance, which hopefully will do much for British hockey. I could not single out any one player. They were all magnificent."

Royal spectator

Hopes of an appearance in the final had been dashed a few days earlier, when, in the presence of the Princess Royal, Germany's two wingers, Heike Latzsch and Nadine Ernsting performed brilliantly to give their team a 2-1 victory. The winning goal came 10 minutes before the end. In the final, Spain beat Germany 2-1 in a tense, but exciting game. Despite only being seeded seventh and being overlooked by much of the media, women's hockey is a much stronger sport in Britain than the male version and their upstaging of the men's team may bring some more publicity to their game.

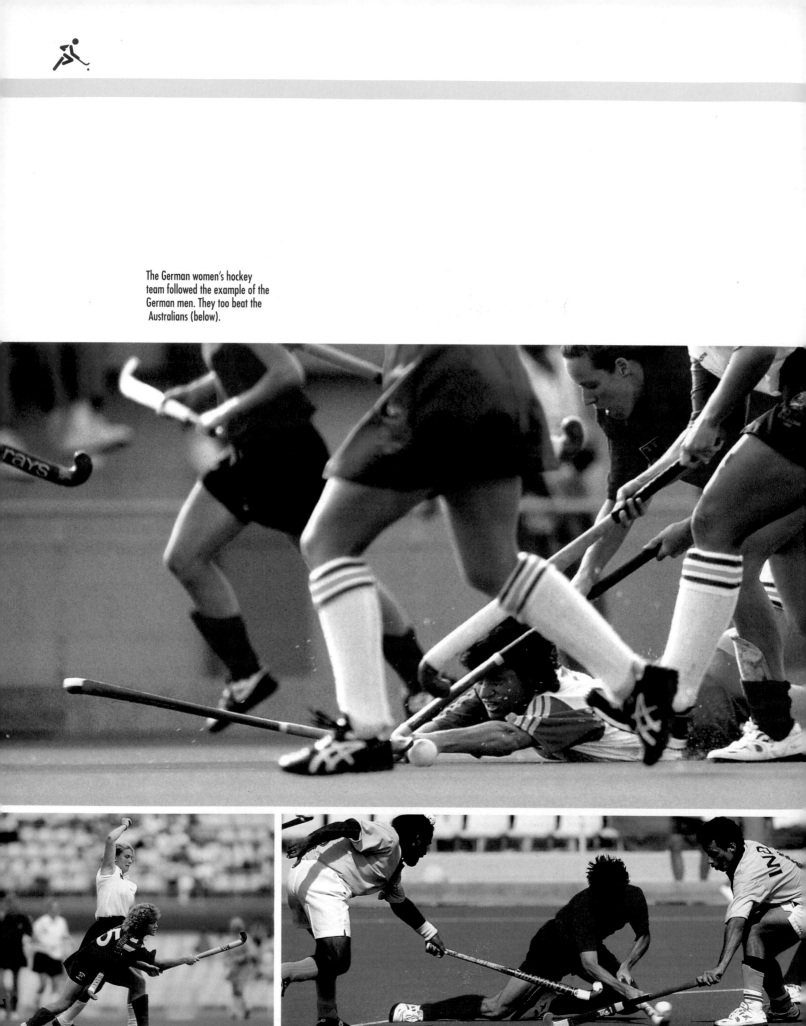

The German women's hockey team followed the example of the German men. They too beat the Australians (below).

A welcome boost

The women's team medal will be a welcome boost to the hockey world given that the last few years have not been the most successful. Britain had re-emerged as a force in world hockey at the Los Angeles Olympics in 1984. The bronze medal was the first medal in the sport for 60 years.

Gold in Seoul for the men

The team had consolidated well in the following four years, so that, at the time of the Seoul Olympics in 1988, Great Britain was one of the strong favourites to win the tournament. Despite the psychological disadvantage of losing to the Germans in the group matches, they beat them in the final. The final drew a large television audience despite starting at about 6.30 am British time.

Tough opposition

For 1992, apart from the good fortune of meeting the group's weakest team, Egypt, as their first opponents and the possibility of a morale-building early victory, the rest of the odds seemed stacked against them. With only two teams qualifying from their group, consisting of Germany, Australia, India, Egypt and Argentina, Great Britain's chances of reaching the semi-finals seemed to be below average. Germany had great strength within their squad and had not lost to Britain in the seven matches played since the 1988 final. The Australians were the Olympic champions prior to the British. India have been Olympic champions eight times and are now re-emerging as a major force. Against such strong opposition, so early in the competition, it seemed Britain would have to overturn pre-tournament form to retain their title, and might well have to settle for a lesser medal. The British team started well, with a 2-0 victory over Egypt, the goals coming from Kerly's 'heir apparent' Rob Hill. This was followed, however, by defeat at the hands of the Germans. Of course, all the talk was about Seoul, when Britain had lost to Germany in the pool matches and then gone on to beat them in the final. But Britain then fell to Australia by the overwhelming score of 6-1.

Psychological blow

Thus denied a medal, the British team's confidence was shattered for their play-off match against Spain, which they lost 2-1. This was a particularly damaging defeat. They are now sixth in world ranking. This means that, for the next four years, Great Britain no longer qualifies automatically for the major tournaments, Norman Hughes, the British coach, will have to juggle the dual problems of rebuilding a weakened team, and succeeding in the qualification matches. The only words of optimism from the British camp as the Games wound down was that the winners, Germany, and the runners-up, Australia, were the only teams to beat them in the group matches. With an excellent crop of young talent coming through, things can only get better.

The Pakistani hockey team have won the Olympic title three times and they put an end to the Dutch team's hopes (above).

Franziska Hentschel in a duel with Johnson (far left).

The German men got off to a good start beating the Indian men 3-0 (middle left).

Victory was within the grasp of the Germans, but the Spanish women were fractionally stronger (left).

Million dollar wedding present

The Olympic badminton court (right). IOC President, Juan Samaranch awards the first gold medal for this event to Indonesia's Susi Susanti (top right).

Badminton has joined tennis and table tennis on the Olympics racket sport menu. After years of pushing, particularly from Malaysia and Indonesia, where badminton is the national sport, it now enjoys full Olympic status. The Indonesian pair, Susi Susanti and her boyfriend, Allan Budi Kusuma, delayed their wedding, so that they could make it to Barcelona and they then successfully saw off all opposition in both badminton singles titles. There will be celebrations in their homeland, as the couple secured Indonesia's first gold medals in any sport after 40 years of trying. The two Indonesians were promised a million dollars by their government after their spectacular double gold. Malaysia also made their mark in the Olympic movement, securing their first ever Olympic medal, winning bronze in the men's doubles. China, world badminton champions, won no gold medals and Britain's best hopes failed to make any impression against the far eastern challenge. Helen Troke, Britain's most successful singles player, suffered a crushing defeat at the hands of World Champion Tang Jiuhong in a game which lasted only 14 minutes. Gill Clark and Julie Bradbury notched up a fine win against an Indonesian pair and raised British medal hopes, but were eliminated in the quarter finals. The South Koreans took both golds in the doubles competitions. The Olympic authorities will be pleased with the first badminton tournament, which attracted impressive television viewing figures.

The road to defeat (left and below). Ardy Wiranata goes down at the hands of his fellow-countryman Allan Budi Kusuma.

Confirmation. Ardy Wiranata, 2nd in the world rankings, won the silver medal.

Alan Budi Kusuma, king of the shuttlecock, celebrates after collecting his gold medal. His girl-friend won the women's event.

BASKETBALL

The 'dream team' shows its form

Send them their medals in advance! The US basketball team were firm favourites from the outset.

There they were at the medal ceremony, beaming like little children. Twelve millionaires who had got together to fulfil a childhood dream. They had been dubbed the 'dream team' and had become one of the major attractions of the Games. Megastars, the best ever, gods – no superlative was spared for the basketball players from the United States.

Even at the end there was no consensus about the exact role they had played in the great Olympic show. Were they the true Olympians, taking part to celebrate their sport, to please the crowd with their skills? Were they merely narcissistic showmen, milking the world's adulation? Or even spoilsports, ruining

US star, Michael Jordan, in an incident from the match against Puerto Rica.

the tournament as a competitive event?

The best of the best

In the past, the United States had always sent a selection of college players to the Olympic basketball tournament. This time, the best players from the best league in the world had joined force to take part. But did this enhance or devalue the tournament? Not even their opponents could agree. "The organizers might as well have sent them their gold medals in advance," commented one of Croatia's star players, Dino Radja. But Detlef Schrempf, the German who has become a world-class player in the United States, argued that it was a marvellous experience for all basketball players to play against this superteam: "Even I was nervous!"

All change

Whatever the rights and wrongs, the 'dream team' was ensured an easy ride now that the Soviet Union and Yugoslavia, two former basketball superpowers, have fallen apart. Opponents became fans who willingly accepted their roles as sacrificial lambs even before the first jump-off. The first game, against Angola, was a farce. The American team was clearly pacing itself for later matches, and at no point made a serious attempt to play hard. The half-time score was 64–16. Before this exhibition tur-

They worked their magic and were fêted as heroes

Even Detlef Schrempf, a German who plays in the American league, could do nothing about the American's overwhelming superiority.

ned into a joke, the Americans saw sense and put their second string on court. The final result of 116–46 was at least presentable.

The game against Germany took a similar course. The German coach, Svetislav Pesic, treated the occasion more as a valuable training session for his players than a proper match. All the players, including the substitutes, were given a chance. And, apart from Detlef Schrempf, they were all overawed. Schrempf, it seemed, was the only one who could live with the Americans. But afterwards he put his performance into perspective: "If the Americans had wanted to cut me out of the game, they could have done so." Henning Harnisch's comment was typical: "It was a pity that Magic Johnson was injured. It would have been great to play against him." They were all happy with their role as extras. They were no more than that, not even good sparring partners.

Croatia went ahead

On only one occasion did we see anything approaching a contest - in the final against Croatia. People paid up to $3000 for tickets on the black market. The Croats wanted to give at least some value for money, for the crowd and for their own self-respect. Captained by the great Drazen Petrovic – who has been playing professionally in the United States for the last two years – they even went ahead midway through the first half. It was the only time in the whole tournament that the 'dream team' lagged behind. By half-

A mêlée of arms and bodies under the net. Germany were defeated by the Unified Team (right).

Detlef Schrempf (right) showed his class. He plays for the Indiana Pacers.

Barkley was playing the 'bad boy'(left). 'Magic' Johnson was the darling of the Games (below).

Detlef Schrempf on the floor (middle). 'Air' Jordan donned the US flag for the medals ceremony.

'Magic' Johnson seduces the Spaniards

'Magic' Johnson charmed the crowds wherever he went and was often greeted with a standing ovation.

time, the Americans had long since restored the order of things and were leading 56–42. In the second half, the crowd were able to feast their eyes on another dazzling display. And the Croats were happy with their silver medal.

Michael 'Air' Jordan, Chris Mullin and Patrick Ewing had won Olympic golds as members of the college-based US team in 1984. Together with Earvin 'Magic' Johnson (the star who recently announced he is HIV positive), Larry Bird, Karl Malone and Charles Barkley, they seduced the basketball-mad Spanish crowd into unbridled hero-worship. Their presence even compensated for the failure of the home team.

Epi, the Spanish basketball hero

In Spain, basketball players are almost as popular as the football stars. Nothing symbolised their status more clearly than the honour given one of them at the opening ceremony. Juan Antonio San Epifano, known throughout Spain as Epi, was allowed to carry the Olympic torch. Playing in his fourth Olympics, he could do nothing to stop the team's disappointing performance, however. It only achieved ninth place. Things went wrong from the beginning, with a defeat against Germany in the first game. The Germans had come with their best team ever and thought they had an outside chance of a medal. Seventh place was a bit of a disappointment, but still their best-ever Olympic result.

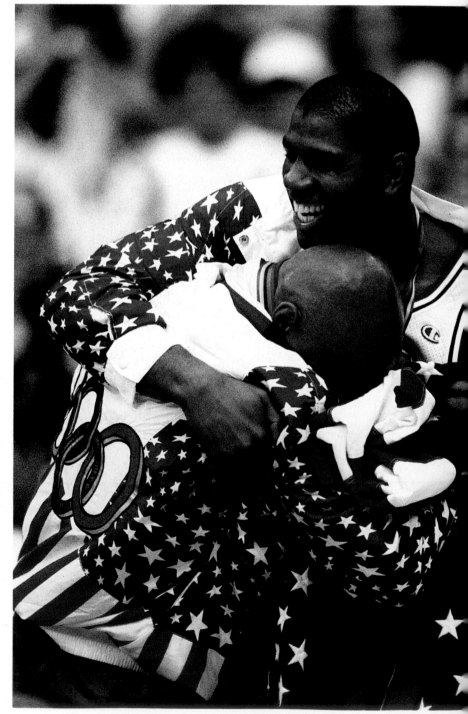

The Unified Team's basketball team were to leave the arena with a heavy heart. It was the end of an era.

The American women came third in the women's event. They had won the event in Seoul and Los Angeles (below).

The Barcelona Games were to be the farewell tour for 'Magic' Johnson (left) and the 'Bird-man' Larry Bird.

197

Action-packed scenes from the men's final. Sweden (below) played the Unified Team (below). Good reason to celebrate (far right)

A disconsolate German team after their defeat (above) at the hands of the eventual winners.

A powerful performance combined with close marking gave the South Koreans victory against Norway in the final.

The end of an era

On the podium stood a bunch of young men who looked as though they had just struck a fearful blow against the Establishment. Whether shaven-headed, bleached blonde, dreadlocked or sporting ear-rings, they waved their national flag around triumphantly. They grinned, they laughed, they looked happy and cheerful, in fact they looked as though they had just won an Olympic championship. But in reality, the bunch of French handball players had only won the bronze medal after defeating the Icelandic team. But their victory had delivered a shock to the handball hierarchy and was cause enough for their unseemly celebrations. On the other side of the podium stood the losers. World champions, Sweden, had won the silver. But if you lose the final, which you ought to have won, there's very little to get excited about. In one of the best handball games in the tournament, the Swedish team had gone under by the slenderest of margins. Both teams deserved gold. In the end, the greater attacking strength of the Unified Team and in particular, the amazingly talented Dushebayev paid off for the Olympic title-holders. It was the last performance of a team which, as the former USSR, had dominated the handball world. While an era had ended in the men's game, for the women, something which was in the air in Seoul, a new trend was confirmed. The restless South Koreans repeated the success of 1988 and finally put paid to European dominance in the sport.

Teamwork is the essence of handball. The South Korean women's team perform a gesture of co-operation and harmony after their victory in the final.

Samba men see off Uncle Sam

Nobody had expected them to be able to do it. But with their characteristic samba rhythms, they soon set the world of volleyball alight. Brazil simply danced and dived into undisputed first place. These Games turned the world of international volleyball completely upside down. Not a single one of the top favourites made it into the final.

American have succeeded only once.

Volleyball is an American invention, but Olympic success was a long time coming. Before 1984, only once was an American team good enough to even qualify for the Games. But in Los Angeles, they came good at last, beating the Brazilians in the men's final. Britain has failed to qualify in either event.

Both finalists were unfancied

In the final, Brazil faced the Netherlands. Both nations had hitherto been seen as outsiders. But the Netherlands never had any real chance of winning this contest. Brazil took the first set 15:12. The attacking play of the South Americans was cunningly varied. Even the manner in which they smashed the ball into the opposing side's court, as they leapt into the air, was enough to intimidate their opponents. Given the force with which the Brazilians played, the Netherlands hardly ever managed to get possession of the ball. Moreover,

the South American players mostly mounted their attack from the rear of the court, leaving little scope for any kind of aggressive play from their opponents.

Height was not a factor

Nor was the Netherlands side ultimately much helped by the superior physical size of its players, (on average, they were about 5" taller than the opposition). The Brazilians managed to win both of the next two sets by a comfortable margin (15:8, 15:5). And immediately after match point, the players, fans, team and their helpers stormed the court. They rolled around the pitch in a mêlée of rejoicing, waving the national flag and dancing the samba all around the Palau Sant Jordi.

The block which the Dutch team had previously deployed so effectively was of little help against the attacking Brazilians (far left).

The Brazilian players dancing for joy having won the gold medal. The Palau Sant Jordi stadium was sold out (below).

American team in shaved head protest

The Dutch could do nothing to counteract the Brazilian's devastating smash shot (above).

USA fail in hat-trick bid

The USA, as the defending champions, had hoped to be the first team to achieve a hat-trick after their gold medal wins in Seoul and Los Angeles. Instead, they had to be content with a bronze. Earlier on in the Games, they had shaved their heads in protest at the refusal to recognise their victory against the Japanese side. By the time of their match against Cuba, their hair had grown into an aggressive-looking short stubble. Perhaps it helped them to achieve their win over

the Cubans by three sets to one. Worse still was the fate of the Italian world champions, who had come to Barcelona in an optimistic mood but ended up in fifth place. The similarities with their performance in the football were striking. For here, too, the southern Europeans could derive no benefit from having the strongest professional side.

Cuban women score direct hit

Cuban success in the women's volleyball was heavily reliant on

one star player - Mireya Luis. The 24-year-old beauty with her strong patriotism for her socialist homeland was the absolute star performer in this discipline. The force of her attacks left even the CIS players in the final almost completely defenceless. At last she had felt genuinely challenged, the Cuban captain announced afterwards, and this was by no means simply a case of showing off. "We came to Barcelona to get the gold," Cuba's coach Eugenio Lafita had said. And that's what you call a direct hit.

Keeping an eye on their opponents, the Cuban women volleyball team had been preparing for the Olympics for a long time (below).

Both on the attack (above) and defending (left), the Cuban's were invincible. Here they are in action against the Brazilian women.

The German men's hockey team repeated their Munich triumph in Barcelona.

The skills of the Brazilian volleyball team were too much for the Dutch squad. Afterwards, the Brazilian supporters danced the samba around the stadium.

Nothing was going to stop the so-called American 'dream team' with stars such as Michael 'Air' Johnson. The Croatian team were the only team to offer any resistance.

Handball

Men	08.08.1992

1. EUN
2. SWE (Sweden)
3. FRA (France)
4. ISL (Iceland)
5. ESP (Spain)
6. USA

Volleyball

Men	09.08.1992

1. BRA (Brazil)
2. NED (Netherlands)
3. USA
4. CUB (Cuba)
5. ITA (Italy)
6. JPN (Japan)

Basketball

Men	08.08.1992

1. USA
2. CRO (Croatia)
3. LIT (Lithuania)
4. EUN
5. BRA (Brazil)
6. AUS (Australia)

Hockey

Men	08.08.1992

1. GER (Germany)
2. AUS (Australia)
3. PAK (Pakistan)
4. NED (Netherlands)
5. ESP (Spain)
6. GBR (Great Britain)

Baseball

	05.08.1992

1. CUB (Cuba)
2. TPE (Taipeh)
3. JPN (Japan)
4. USA

Football

	08.08.1992

1. ESP (Spain)
2. POL (Poland)
3. GHA (Ghana)
4. AUS (Australia)

Badminton-singles

Men	04.08.1992

1. A. B. Kusuma (INA)
2. A. Wiranata (INA)
3. T. Stuer-Lauridsen (DEN)
3. H. Susanto (INA)

Badminton-doubles

Men	04.08.1992

1. Moon.Soo Kim · Joo Bong Park (PRK)
2. Hartono · Gunawan (INA)
3. Sidek · Sidek (MAL)
3. Yonbo Li · Bingyi Tian (CHN)

Tennis-doubles

Men	07.08.1992

1. B. Becker · S. Stich (GER)
2. W. Ferreira · P. Norval (RSA)
3. J. Frana · C. Miniussi (ARG)
3. G. Ivanisevic · G. Prpic (CRO)

Tennis-singles

Men	07.08.1992

1. M. Rosset (SUI)
2. J. Arrese (ESP)
3. G. Ivanisevic (CRO)
3. A. Cherkasov (EUN)

Quarter finals

Rosset · Sanchez	3-1
Ivanisevic · Santoro	3-2
Cherkasov · Oncins	3-2
Arrese · Lavalle	3-0

Table tennis-doubles

Men	04.08.1992

1. Lu Lin · Wang Tao (CHN)
2. Roßkopf · Fetzner (GER)
3. Yoo Nam Kyu · Kim Tae Boo (KOR)
3. Kang Hee Chan · Lee Chul Seu (KOR)

Table tennis-singles

Men	06.08.1992

1. J.-O. Waldner (SWE)
2. J.-P. Gatien (FRA)
3. Kim Taek Soo (KOR)
3. Ma Wenge (CHN)

Quarter finals

Gatien · Yi Ding	3-2
Ma Wenge · Persson	3-0
Kim Taek Soo · Tao Wang	3-1
Waldner · Roßkopf	3-1

An unforgettable moment. The Brazilian team celebrated in dramatic style after their volleyball victory.

Hong Quia (CHN) took gold in the singles and doubles table tennis. He was one of the many successful far-eastern players.

Mary-Joe and Gigi Fernandez (USA) beat the local favourites, Sanchez and Martinez for the gold medal in the women's doubles.

Handball

Women	08.08.1992
1. KOR (South Korea)	
2. NOR (Norway)	
3. EUN	
4. GER (Germany)	
5. AUT (Austria)	
6. USA	

Volleyball

Women	08.08.1992
1. CUB (Cuba)	
2. EUN	
3. USA	
4. BRA (Brazil)	
5. JPN (Japan)	
6. NED (Netherlands)	

Basketball

Women	07.08.1992
1. EUN	
2. CHN (China)	
3. USA	
4. CUB (Cuba)	
5. ESP (Spain)	
6. TCH (Czechoslovakia)	

Hockey

Women	08.08.1992
1. ESP (Spain)	
2. GER (Germany)	
3. GBR (Great Britain)	
4. KOR (South Korea)	
5. AUS (Australia)	
6. NED (Netherlands)	

Tennis-doubles

Women	08.08.1992
1. Fernandez · Fernandez (USA)	
2. Sanchez-V. · Martinez (ESP)	
3. Meshki · Zvereva (EUN)	
3. McQuillan · Provis (AUS)	

Badminton-singles

Women	04.08.1992
1. S. Susanti (INA)	
2. Soon Hyun Bang (KOR)	
3. H. Huang (CHN)	
3. J. Tang (CHN)	

Badminton-doubles

Women	04.08.1992
1. Hy-Young Hwang · So-Young Chun (KOR)	
2. Guan · Qunhua Nong (CHN)	
3. Young-Ah Gil · Eun-Jung Shim (KOR)	
3. Lin · Yao (CHN)	

Tennis singles

Women	07.08.1992
1. J. Capriati (USA)	
2. S. Graf (GER)	
3. M.-J. Fernandez (USA)	
3. A. Sanchez-Vicario (ESP)	

Quarter finals	
Graf · Appelmans	2-0
Fernandez · Maleeva	2-1
Capriati · Huber	2-0
Sanchez-V. · Martinez	2-0

Table tennis-singles

Women	05.08.1992
1. Y. Deng (CHN)	
2. H. Quiao (CHN)	
3. Jung Hyun (KOR)	
3. Bun Li (PRK)	

Quarter finals	
Deng · Yu	3-0
Jung Hyun · Ciosu	3-2
Bun Li · Chen	3-1
Quiao · Chai	3-0

Table tennis-doubles

Women	03.08.1992
1. Y. Deng · H. Qiao (CHN)	
2. Z. Chen · J. Gao (CHN)	
3. Bun Li · Sun Yu (PRK)	
3. Cha Hong · Jung Hyun (KOR)	

US ESPEREM A ...
OS ESPERAMOS EN ...
RENDEZ-VOUS À ...
SEE YOU IN ...

ATLANTA '96

Project Leader
ROLAND M. GÖÖCK
Assistant
DORIS BUCHHOLZ

Concept
MICHAEL EPPINGER

Edited by
UPS TRANSLATIONS
London
Assistant Editor
PAUL G. FLETCHER

Art Direction
SPORTARTS, Hamburg

Art Co-ordinator
MAJA MORITZ
Assistant
BRIGITTE SCHALLER
CHRISTIAN HRUSCHKA

Photography
BONGARTS, Hamburg

LUTZ BONGARTS
HENNING BANGEN
ALEXANDER HASSENSTEIN
HENRI SZWARC
STEPHAN RISSMANN

Lithography
HANS-DIETER STÖNNER
ANITA MUND

Typesetting
MANFRED ROTHER

Printed and bound by
MOHNDRUCK
Graphische Betriebe GmbH
Gütersloh

Paper
GARDAMATT
Cartiere del Garda, Riva

ISBN 3-576-80005-0
Printed in Germany